SEVEN SEVENS

A Miscellany

BY THE SAME AUTHOR

OLIVER AND BOYD
 Let's Ask the Padre – Broadcast Talks
 The Padre Presents – Broadcast Discussions
 Our Club – The Boys' Club in the Canongate
 The Order of Divine Service
 The Kirk in the Canongate

LONGMANS, GREEN
 The Average Man – Broadcast Talks
 The Greater Victory – Broadcast Talks
 Small Talks – Broadcast Talks

OXFORD UNIVERSITY PRESS
 Asking Why (with A. W. Loos)
 Take Up God's Armour – Talks to Schools and Colleges

WILLIAM BLACKWOOD & SONS LTD.
 The Morning Service on the Lord's Day
 Roses in December – Broadcast Talks
 The Seven Dwarfs – Broadcast Talks
 Haply I May Remember – Broadcast Talks
 In Christ We Are All One – Moderator's Address

GEOFFREY BLES
 The Beloved Captain – Donald Hankey's Essays

THE EPWORTH PRESS
 Whatever the Years – Broadcast Talks
 What Worries Me – Broadcast Selections
 Great Men – Broadcast Talks

LAYMEN (PUBLICATIONS) LTD.
 They Looked Unto Him – Broadcast Talks
 The Selfsame Miracles – Broadcast Talks

Edited:

OXFORD UNIVERSITY PRESS
 Asking Them Questions – First Series
 Asking Them Questions – Second Series
 Soldiers Also Asked
 Asking Them Questions – Third Series
 Asking Them Questions – A Selection
 Fathers of the Kirk
 A Manual of Church Doctrine (with T. F. Torrance)
 Asking Them Questions – New Series I
 Asking Them Questions – New Series II

ALLENSON
 I Attack

HODDER AND STOUGHTON
 Front Line Religion
 Studdert-Kennedy's Why
 Aren't All the Best Chaps Christians?

SEVEN SEVENS

A Miscellany

Ronald Selby Wright

1977

Scottish Academic Press

Edinburgh

Published by
Scottish Academic Press Ltd.
33 Montgomery Street, Edinburgh EH7 5JX

Distributed by
Chatto and Windus Ltd.
40 William IV Street
London WC2N 4DF

ISBN 7073 0139 4

Printed in Great Britain by
R. & R. Clark, Ltd., Edinburgh

Contents

Dedicated by gracious permission

To

HIS ROYAL HIGHNESS
PRINCE CHARLES, K.G., K.T., G.M.B.

Prince of Wales and Great Steward of Scotland

Preface

I was called in November 1936 and the following January was inducted to the Canongate Kirk (The Kirk of Holyroodhouse) in the Royal Mile of Edinburgh; and though I was away during the years of war as an army chaplain and Radio Padre, I have known no other parish.

How changed are these present days from those when I first came to this old historic downtown parish, from those I knew in 1927, the year I started our Club for the boys (which still continues, though on a much smaller scale) right through the earlier part of my ministry. These were times of deep depression, overcrowding (sometimes as many as seven people in one room – their only home), unemployment on a vast scale, real poverty; but borne with a cheerfulness and courage and kindness that knew no equal, except perhaps in the years of war.

As I write, the face of the parish has completely changed. Slowly but surely the new housing areas took over many of the overcrowded homes; old buildings were either demolished, restored or re-built, and every house has its own kitchen, bathroom and other rooms besides. Where once there were three thousand children in the parish when first I came, now there are not more than one hundred and fifty – from the nursery school to school leavers. Where once there was a boys' choir of fifty, now there is none; and a Sunday school of five hundred children is now but a handful.

Since 1888 there have been only two Ministers in this parish. My predecessor, who went as the Assistant Minister in 1886, became Minister two years later and remained until his retirement and death in 1936. In the last ninety years only two Ministers!

All the talks or incidents in this book have in one form or another been heard within the parish church at some time or another, but many too have been broadcast, some of them in the days when I was Radio Padre. Some have appeared in booklet form at the request of listeners; but though all are now out of print, I still get requests for some talk that is no longer available. Others, like the school sermons, have not been in print previously, though in 1967 the Oxford Univer-

sity Press published a volume of my school addresses under the title of
Take Up God's Armour. Not only have I had the privilege of being the
Minister of my own Church and the added privilege of talking to men
(and women) of the army, navy and air force, in their various stations
at home and abroad and at Sandhurst, Dartmouth and Cranwell, I
have also visited and spoken, through the kind invitation of their Head
Masters, to many schools and colleges throughout the United Kingdom. In these schools, in H.M. forces, and in my Boys' Club and
camps from 1927 to this day I have had the great joy of meeting and
speaking to many young people; and though it has ever been the
custom to think that young people were never as good as the last
generation, I feel more than ever that most of the present young
generation are much more considerate and compassionate and thought-
ful than we were in our time. The consideration shown by young
people for old people, for the "third world" (I am not quite sure
where the second world is!) and for causes that bring out their compassion and concern for ordinary justice, is never emphasised enough
today. If we do hear more about the "revoltingness" of youth, it is
largely because the small noisy minority are those who make the news
headlines, and that today through the media of radio and television
and the public press, we know more of what is going on than ever was
known before, and too often the wrong going on!

I offer this simple nostalgic miscellany with grateful thanks to all
those who have helped me throughout the years, whose prayers have
sustained me and whose gracious kindnesses have encouraged me,
echoing the view of one of our best Boys' Club leaders who died some
years ago and who said to me shortly before he died, "I don't think I
have done these fellows much good really, but oh the good they have
done me."

When I started in my parish I was looking ahead – forty years on;
now I am looking forty years back! I have loved every minute – or
nearly every minute! – of it, and would gladly start again, with the
same good and dear folk from my home onwards around me, realising
now my many mistakes, but hoping to do oh so much better next
time.

RONALD SELBY WRIGHT

Manse of the Canongate,
Edinburgh.   Lent 1977.

Acknowledgements

I should like to thank Mr Douglas Grant and the publishers and printers for making this book possible, my secretary, Mrs Taylor, for typing and sometimes retyping a not always very easy manuscript, the Rev. Hugh Mackay for his drawings, Mr Harry Richmond and the Revs. Norman Drummond, C.F. and Henry Kirk for their interest and encouragement; I also appreciate the helpful advice given me by Mr Douglas Blackwood and Mr J. R. Snowball.

My thanks too are due to Mrs G. B. Gibbs for her permission to publish the poem on page 87 and to Walt Disney Productions for permission to use the copyright drawings of the Seven Dwarfs, and to the *Daily Express* for the photo of my dog, Gen, and myself.

My debts to others should be obvious; and if I have unwittingly infringed any copyright either by paraphrase or by quotation, I hope they will forgive me. The late Dr Charles Warr, to whom I owe so much, once reminded us that Fr Stanton is said to have whimsically remarked that he disliked publishing his sermons since people recognised how much he owed to Spurgeon! It is the Stantons, Warrs and MacLeods rather than the Spurgeons of this world to whom I owe most.

Any profit from this work will go to our Club – the Boys' Club in the Canongate, which in a sense started it all for me fifty years ago.

R.S.W.

Seven Saints

These talks on seven of my favourite Saints were given at different times and under different circumstances. Some were broadcast at the early morning Daily Service, that on St. Andrew was delivered first at St. Columba's, Pont Street, London, at a St. Andrew's Day Service and later broadcast, and has been used since at Loretto School. The talk on St. Margaret, Queen of Scotland, is a shorter version of that given at her 900th Anniversary at the Service at Queensferry near Edinburgh. The talks on St. Francis Xavier and St. Francis of Assisi are both based on earlier Radio Padre talks.

St. Margaret, Queen of Scotland
(c. 1050–1093)

It all came about in a strange way, and indeed one can say that the Norman Conquest of England led to the Saxon conquest of a Scottish King, and indeed to the Roman conquest of the Scottish Church. Malcolm Canmore whose father Duncan had been murdered by Macbeth, had spent seventeen years as an exile in England before his victory over Macbeth and his Coronation at Scone. On that date we all remember – 1066 – Harold, the King of England was killed at the Battle of Hastings and his heir Edgar fled for refuge to Hungary as he thought, but owing to a providential storm, to Scotland; and so it happened that up the coast of Fife there came an English ship which landed a Royal list of passengers, including the heir to the throne of England, and the Princesses Margaret and Christina. They were hurried to Dunfermline, these royal guests, where they were met by King Malcolm who welcomed them and gave them hospitality.

And so it was that King Malcolm met his future Queen again (for years before they must have met at the English Court) – now about twenty years old – Margaret. Malcolm was said to be a fairly rough and not too cultured man, and his conquest of the Princess Margaret was more difficult than his conquest of Macbeth. Brought up under the rule of St. Benedict she had intended indeed to be a nun, but seeing the great interest that the King of Scotland was taking in her, she sought the guidance of her spiritual adviser Turgot and, who knows, but that his advice was that given so long before, that there must have been some purpose in her being called to be a Queen and that she must realise in that purpose the part she had to play and the words of Mordecai might well have rung in her heart, "Who knoweth whether thou art not come to the kingdom for such a time as this?"[1]

[1] Esther 4: 14.

So it was that the Princess Margaret of England became Queen
Margaret of Scotland and brought with her all her devout culture that
had been hers from her earliest days, and found both a home and a
crown in Scotland. Here she could devote all her life to God's service
though in a different way from what she had earlier contemplated as
a nun; here was a different but greater opportunity of fulfilling her
life's desire; and Malcolm worshipped her so much that he loved and
respected all that she did. Once again we turn to Turgot, "There was
in him a sort of fear of offending one whose life was so venerable; for
he had perceived that Christ dwelt truly in her heart. He hastened to
obey her wishes and prudent counsels in all things. Whatever she refused, he refused also; whatever pleased her, he also loved for the love
of her." Ever the fierce, rough soldier, he now also became a man
with ability of purpose and a kindless of heart. She taught her children
herself along with all her other duties, and Scotland began to see a
new conception of what a Christian should be. It is to one of these
eight children, King David, that we owe in Scotland one of the
greatest increases in its Church in the 12th century, and this he had
learnt first at his mother's knee. Wherever she went she took with her
her copy of the Gospels, the original of which is now in the Bodleian
Library in Oxford, and a copy of which, gifted by the late Sir David
Russell, is now in St. Margaret's Chapel in Edinburgh Castle; and all
she learnt there she passed on. True, she got rid of the Celtic Church
and brought Scotland under the rule of Rome. This would not have
been easy had she not been the person she was. And so Scotland
changed her date for Easter, her marriage laws, and began now to
treat the Lord's Day as the Day of Worship and rest from labour, and
altered the type of service. She pioneered for unity of the church, but
with all that she sought the unity of her people; each day we are told
the poor would come to the royal hall, where she herself fed them and
gave them a drink, with the King beside her. Each day we are told,
she, following our Lord's example, washed the feet of twenty-four
poor men; and the ladies of the Court had to join her in helping to
make clothes for the poor and needy; for so did Scotland begin to
learn again the meaning of God's love through her Queen; and as
people began to travel to Dunfermline or St. Andrews, two names
were added to the map of Scotland, Queensferry and St. Margaret's
Hope. A saint she was in the true sense of the word and a saint later
she was made by the Church. As Mgr. Knox once put it, "Thus she

may be fairly regarded as the Patron Saint of wives, who have in these days much need of a Patron Saint!"

Someone once defined a Christian as "one who makes it easier for others to believe in God". This she did for Scotland and brought a new light into her darkness. People through her began to find it easier to believe in God and Scotland began to win a name for which she has been known throughout the civilised world, as a country of faith, with a love of true learning and a concern for all men.

Each week in her Chapel in Edinburgh Castle, the Margarets of Scotland still remember her, still "keep her memory green". But the best and surest way we can all remember her is, surely, to try to practice some of her gracious and kindly ways as very ordinary simple Christian people, and so try to make it "easier for others to believe in God". And even such simple ordinary folk like you and me can at least try.

St. Francis of Assisi
(1182–1226)

The first time I saw Assisi was on a never-to-be-forgotten morning in spring. I had crossed the Apennines from Bari to Naples, travelled the famous Appian Way to Rome and then on to Perugia. There, from my window, I strained my eyes across the plains, but when I arrived it was late evening, and till the morning this promised land lay hidden. In the morning I set out, and, shortly after starting, I saw Assisi through the early morning mist of the Umbrian Plain, a "city set on a hill", truly

"... a city such as vision builds ..."

I have returned to it several times since and I feel that, were I to stay there always, I'd never weary of the place.

And now, in a mind stored with memories, some of the happiest I've got are of walking with friends to St. Damian's or the Carceri – that lovely little monastery where still the tree stands where

Francis, they say, preached to the birds; or going for the first time, and alone, to his tomb in the lower chapel of the great three-storied Church which is his sepulchre. How beautiful are the blossoms there in spring; but in summer, though the lovely blossoms have gone, there is a new beauty there – the haze of the summer days rising from the Umbrian Plains, the warm comfort of the sun, the ripening fruits.

The place is unscarred by the havoc of war, for both friend and foe have honoured and kept safe from harm this place so dear to all who love this troubadour of God who now can truly be called "Everyman's Saint".

His father was a prosperous business man – an Assisi merchant, whose business sometimes took him into other lands. And it was while he was in France that his son was born, so he called him "Frenchy", from which we get the name Francis.[2]

None could have expected how the gay young blood of Assisi would turn out – the laughing sportsman, the leader of the smart set, this very much-loved young man, who showed, too, that he had no mean head for business. At times, he did some rather odd things – gave a pretty good coat once to a beggar on the road. Yet perhaps not so odd – for most fellows do things like that really when it comes to the bit. It's true he did behave rather strangely when he was a prisioner of war. He was so decent to everyone, especially to those who, for one reason or another, were out of the usual circle. Much as Rangers travel north to play Aberdeen, so, in these days, did Assisi set out to fight Perugia or some other city round about, and Francis played for the home team. A prisoner of war in Perugia, Francis was now allowed a certain amount of free time in which to think of his future. What a great future it would be! He had wealth, he had gifts, he had popularity, he had . . . "I shall be loved by all the world" – that was his future. So laughing, he rode back to Assisi and to his happy life. But he found the lights lowered, business seemed less absorbing, fun seemed less funny, gaiety less gay. He was twenty-one.

But during his convalescence after an illness immediately following his return, the lights went up again, only to go out as on his first day out he gazed from the Porta Nouva across the slopes of the

[2] In Sabatier's life, he likens the century in which Francis lived, to a young man of twenty, and the Church had become old-fashioned and "unable to hold youth" and most of the usual jargon we hear today. "Then Francis came and the world saw that the Church had perennial youth."

Umbrian Hills. The journey back home from that gate was his first
step to the Francis we know and love.[3]

Life would always be fun for Francis, life would always be happy.
The reason why the fun and gaiety seemed to have gone was not
because they were wrong, but because he had discovered that life must
have purpose and direction, and only in the seeking and the finding of
the right purpose and direction would the true joy of life come.

He hadn't quite got the answer yet, though. Perhaps, he thought,
he ought to do something big – go on a crusade or something. Well,
he was lucky, there was one due to set off very soon. Grand. So he
tried on his best armour; but before the Crusade had set out he had
given it away to a poor fellow in a poor suit, and, before the Crusade
was a few days old, the once gallant young man of Assisi was on his
way home. A dream, his conscience, or maybe his imagination, told
him that this was not really the way. And so he came back. The
Colonel Blimps of Assisi said, of course, that it was quite "monstrous";
but some of the younger people, who still flocked around him,
thought it might be love.

"That's what he needs", said all the old ladies of Assisi, "a wife
that will settle him down a bit – I do hope he gets a nice girl and not
that awful Charlotta girl" – and so on, with the usual conversation
that goes on still in the 20th century. Meanwhile, all the time Francis
is trying to see ahead, and to conquer those things he feared most –
lepers and haunting eyes of the poor; and all the time the gossiping
went on about him.

Now Francis, like so many cheerful young fellows today, was
quite a good churchman; so he thought he'd go and see the parson and
have a talk with him. His parson was the Bishop of Assisi, and he gave
him the kind of advice we too often give people and told him to pull
himself together and all the things he oughtn't to do – you remember
what a certain old woman is reported to have said about the Ten
Commandments – "Them Ten Commandments, they don't get you
anywhere – they only put ideas into your head." Well, the Bishop's
advice didn't get Francis anywhere – and the poor fellow was almost
in a worse state than ever; knowing what he oughtn't to do, he
couldn't think what he ought to do. And Francis tackled his first fear

[3] His message at this time, Fr. Mackay tells us, is just this, "To die for love is a
great adventure. To live for love is a far greater adventure, and this means bringing
love to meet love every day in the common things of life."

by being brought face to face with it. For one day, when riding back from Assisi, he saw a leper standing before him – more, he was coming towards him. Here was a great crisis – he was brought face to face with what he feared most. Spurring his shying horse towards the leper, he leapt from his saddle, put his arms round the rotting body, and kissed the face now almost eaten away by disease. The next day, a stirring crowd of lepers saw a strange sight – the gay young blood of Assisi had not only come to see them, but be their friend. It wasn't that Francis liked it; for though he looked cheerful as he kissed each leprous hand, the chroniclers tell how he nearly fainted with the strain and horror of it.

But having broken through and with a new vision, he went down to the little ruined chapel of St. Damien, and knelt before that large and rather ugly crucifix which you now see in the Church of St. Clare. And there he gave himself to God: "O Lord Jesus, enlighten me, lift my darkness from me. Let me know you so well, that on all things I may act in your light and as you will." And the answer the gay young man of Assisi heard coming from God: "Go and build my falling-down house for me." Well, you know what happened next; Francis took the words literally at first and began to rebuild St. Damiens, and some other Churches around. Meanwhile, he had quarrelled with his father, renounced his heritage, given up his old life, and become a beggar round the houses where he had formerly been a welcome guest – his only friends, the lepers who loved him still. Still singing and still happy, he had finished the restoration of St. Mary of the Angels, and then one day in the year 1209 at the service there, he heard God speak to him in the lesson, "Preach, saying the kingdom of God is at hand. Heal the sick, cleanse the lepers, raise the dead, cast out devils. Freely ye have received, freely give." And dressed now in a grey-brown sacking tunic with a piece of rope for a girdle, he went up to Assisi and right up to the market square where the business men and dignitaries were, and said, "Brothers, the Lord give you peace". And in silence and awe they listened to him. And from that number, a great and wealthy nobleman and a distinguished lawyer threw in their lot with him; later they were joined by a young ploughboy – Giles – who was found looking for Francis in the forest and wondering if he, too, could join them. So the great movement started as a nobleman, a lawyer, and ploughboy and St. Francis shared their bread – all gloriously happy. And the numbers grew. At first the Church didn't

understand it. When nine years later, the hierarchy of the Church sent
a deputation to see them, they saw coming towards them not four, but
five thousand brown-clad brothers. "It is the feast of Pentecost," said
the Cardinal Legate, "and mine eyes behold the army of the Holy
Ghost." And he became lost in the army of the brothers, stripped himself of his robes and became one of them. But others were canny and
more difficult. "I do not understand your rule," said a prince of the
Church, "you'd better take and read it to the pigs." Smiling, Francis
departed to return soon again; "I have read it to the pigs, sir, and they
don't understand it either." Yet the Pope, Innocent III, said, "What
this age needs is the spirit of the Troubadours", and later when his
successor, Pope Honorius, said as he saw him, "There goes a very
dangerous man", and a jealous Cardinal said, "Indeed, I think so,
Holy Father"; but, said Cardinal Ugilino – the one later to join the
order – "but, dangerous to whom, Holy Father?" "To the devil, my
son." So the troubadours of God, led by the Poverello, sang their way
through the world in the name of the Lord, and the world was to see
again the perennial youth of the Church. They loved all things and all
people – they spoke of "our brother the sun, our brother the wind,
our sister water, our brother fire, mother earth" even "sister death".
Even the animals and birds returned the love they showed them – for
love is just like that. And Francis died in his beloved St. Mary of the
Angels, and we read how "then all the larks of the forest rose and
soared. Stretching their wings and tuning their voices, they gathered
in a company above St. Mary of the Angels, and rose into the evening
sky, a circling crown of song."

Before I left Assisi on my last visit, I asked to see the famous letter
that Francis wrote, at the end of his life, to Brother Leo.

At the end of the letter he had drawn a hill shaped like a skull, and
on it a cross which covers the horizon, a cross with no head to it, no
inscription on it.

It is a cross shaped like a hammer

What was his secret? Well, here at least is a clue to close with,
taken from G. K. Chesterton's picture of St. Francis, and which,
incidentally, is a wonderful picture of one of the great secrets of true
leadership.

"What gave him his extraordinary power was this: that from the
Pope to the beggar, from the Sultan of Syria in his pavilion to the
ragged robber crawling out of the wood, there was never a man who

looked into these round eyes without being certain that Francis Bernardone was interested in him, in his own individual life from the cradle to the grave, that he himself was taken and valued seriously."

It is little wonder then that after his death one of his followers once saw him in a vision alone in the pageant of the Church Triumphant to be "walking easily and steadily in the actual footprints of our Lord".

St. Andrew
(1st century A.D.)

As he walked by the Sea of Galilee, he saw two brothers, Simon who is called Peter and Andrew his brother, casting a net into the sea; for they were fishermen. And he said to them, "Follow me, and I will make you fishers of men." Immediately they left their nets and followed him. And going on from there he saw two other brothers, James the son of Zebedee and John his brother, in the boat with Zebedee their father, mending their nets, and he called them. Immediately they left the boat and their father, and followed him.

St. Matthew 4: 18–22

Having read that I invite you to consider three short sentences:
1. "And He allowed no one to go with Him except Peter and James and John, the brother of James."
2. "Six days later Jesus took with Him Peter, James and his brother John and led them up a high mountain where they could be alone."
3. "Then He took Peter and James and John with Him. And a sudden fear came over Him and great distress."

Now what is missing in these three sentences and why? Well, at a glance I am sure you will notice that the name of Andrew is missing; and yet somehow it was Andrew that started it all!

You remember that Andrew was the first and he brought his brother to Jesus. James and John too were brothers, yet it isn't four brothers but three who are mentioned, and Andrew the one left out.

He was, as someone once put it,[4] "the disciple who showed the difficulty of a lack of appreciation of the difficulty". He was the kind of
man you would just like to go and talk to: the young boy who carried
the provisions for the disciples' supper, the boy who carried the five
loaves and two fishes, must have been fond of him. You remember
how when everyone was getting worried about the catering and how
so many were going to be fed with seemingly so little, Andrew came
shoving his way through the crowd, the boy walking along beside
him, and taking the whole thing quite lightheartedly, while James and
John might be saying that they wished he would take things a little bit
more seriously; and how Andrew would turn to them a bit later and
say, "There you are now, none of you ever thought of *that*." And,
after all, he was perfectly right. And remember a time too when those
Greeks came up to Philip and said, "Sir, we would see Jesus", and
how Philip did not know how to go about this, and it was Andrew he
consulted – the most accessible and friendly of the disciples – and quite
typically Andrew saw no difficulty at all, he just told him to come
along and he was quite sure He would speak to him; and once again
he was right.

As well as being the Scottish Patron Saint he became the Patron
Saint of Russia and of Greece and saw no difficulty in going to the
most important people and asking them quite simply to become followers of Christ – as first he had done to his brother. He never saw
any difficulty in anything; but unfortunately sometimes other people
did; and after he had converted the wife of a Pro-Consul, the Pro-
Consul had Andrew scourged and crucified on a Saltire cross that we
now call St. Andrew's Cross, dying quite cheerfully and triumphantly.

The story goes that some of his relics were brought to Scotland by
St. Rule to the town we now call St. Andrews; but it was not for that
reason that he became Patron Saint of Scotland – that was another and
quite different occasion when Angus the Pictish King beat the King of
the Britons, having seen the blue and white Saltire shape in the sky
and taken it as his "banner".

He took everything fairly lightly, even his death. Our Lord died
of a broken heart but St. Andrew, it is said, died triumphantly. Our
Lord spoke seven words from His Cross, and tradition tells us that
St. Andrew preached for two days from his (which may help to
explain why some Scottish ministers' sermons may be so long!). One

[4] H. F. B. Mackay.

can begin to see perhaps some of the reasons why he was left out when the other three were taken. He was never able to see "the greatest heights of vision because he was incapable of the greatest depths of suffering".

Now, it is of course good to have a cheerful outlook and there is a place for it among the disciples, a place among the Saints whom St. Andrew somehow represented, but it alone cannot always do the greatest and deepest service of all. If religion is merely a comfort and relief – a kind of spiritual aspirin to be swallowed once a week – then it is hard to be a full disciple. It's not *enough* to have a sure and happy sense of God's Presence; one must be able to hold on when things are difficult and the outlook unpromising. And one too must also feel at times something of the sorrow which is in the world. But St. Andrew can teach us something very important and very precious – that we should try to serve God faithfully in our own simple way, without bitterness or jealousy.[5]

However disappointed we may sometimes be, discipleship means serving to the end, to try to bring not only our brother but to bring outsiders to Him, and not worry but rather be pleased if they and not us receive a more honoured place, and to see sometimes the hidden good in other people however small may be their offering: "There is a lad here who has not very much, yet . . ." And you and I, God knows, have not very much to give – but if it is all we have it is enough. Let us be ourselves; it doesn't matter if we never get into the limelight or the premier league, so long as we try our best to serve God faithfully and cheerfully to the end, without bitterness or jealousy or worldly ambition; but with sincerity and humility and an infectious faith that leads others to a height that we never can reach in the service of God and man.

[5] I remember Lieut.-General Sir George Gordon Lennox telling me once that when he was at Eton there was a Master whom they all respected and liked so much and who was constantly being asked to preach the sermon, when he was a boy in Lower Chapel. He was eventually persuaded to do so and he got up and said, "Boys, my sermon will be very short – in fact it will be only four words, 'Boys, never be jealous.'" Of all the sermons preached to that generation at Eton that was one that was never forgotten!

St. Patrick
(373–463)

17th March, as every Irishman knows, is St. Patrick's Day; but at least we Scots have this consolation when it comes to St. Patrick, that he was probably a Scotsman too, because he seems to have been born near Dumbarton (and – to be fair about it – don't let us in Scotland forget that our Scottish St. Columba was born in Ireland; which cancels things out a bit!).

In any case great men belong to all the world; there are no nations and races and countries in the eyes of God the great Father of all; all men are His sons, and all men are therefore brothers. And St. Patrick was a great man; and it is right and proper that all men should remember him and honour his memory.

As I have said, he was probably born near Dumbarton about the year 373. His father and mother were both Christians – his father a Roman and his mother probably a niece of the great St. Martin of Tours. And as all good Christian parents should do, they brought up their son in the Christian faith; and like quite a lot of boys then and since, it didn't mean very much to him and he didn't take it very seriously; but the foundation was there, however little he realised it at the time; and it was on that foundation that he was later able to build.

When his father retired the family went to live near St. Ninian at Whithorn; and I like to think that young Patrick met Ninian there and learnt something from him about his mother's uncle St. Martin.

When he was what we would call today "a teenager" of about sixteen, the Scots (as the Irish were then called) made one of their raids (nowadays we are much more civilised and they come to Murrayfield) and young Patrick was captured and taken to Ireland. His father and mother were probably killed.

In Ireland he became a slave to an Irish chief and for a number of years looked after the pigs. A young orphan boy alone on the hills, he remembered what his parents had taught him; and he began to say his prayers again.

Shortly he ran away from his master and went to France and Britain and then Rome; and there the Pope made him a bishop and he returned to the same place in Ireland where he had first landed as a boy captive fourteen years before, only this time he was welcomed by the local chief; and there at what we now call Downpatrick, the first Christian church in Ireland was established and his great missionary work began.

Now there was in Ireland at that time the chief of all the chiefs and he lived in Tara and since that was the centre of the Druid religion Patrick soon realised that before he could do much he must go to Tara. The High King was at first not at all pleased to see Patrick; but when Patrick said that he came in peace the King was greatly impressed by his calm dignity and deep sincerity; and at the request of the King on Easter Day 433 St. Patrick preached the Gospel of Christ in the great hall of Tara.

Thirty-six years later he died; and his statue stands now on Tara hill; and when darkness fell over Europe the light of Patrick still burned bright.

And so, I'd like you to remember him again; to remember the priceless benefits of a Christian home, the abiding comfort of the eternal God who is with us too, whether in the loneliness of the hills or the crowded hall of Tara.

St. Columba
(521–597)

There had been religion on Iona long before Christ was born – for that matter, there has always been religion in the world. The people sought for the unknown God and worshipped the Sun and the Fire; and on Iona the Druids, for such was the name of the priests, made altars of stone and sacrificed to their god and claimed to influence the wind and the weather by means of charms and spells. To many people today Iona still has "another world" feeling, and I think most people when they step on the island get a strange sense of peace: So from the earliest times it has been a Holy Island.

Even in the days when the Druids were offering their sacrifices there, occasional rumours had come of great happenings in Palestine. For the stories of Jesus Christ had begun to reach Britain through such men as Palladius and Ninian.

Then there was a boy born, probably near Dumbarton – a boy called Patrick about whom I have already told you. The King of Ireland had his son Conall baptised by Patrick, and Conall became a good Christian man, and so brought up his family as good Christian people. And the records show that he had a great-grandson whom today we all remember, Columba.

Columba then had the great advantage of coming from a Christian home. Some of you may not be able to do very much for your country, but I don't care how much you can do, you can never do better than have a Christian home. You see, then, St. Columba was of royal blood; but it is not as a royal prince that we remember him today but as a humble follower of the King of Kings.

Indeed, it's quite likely that Columba might have been King of Ireland had he so wished. His mother, who was a princess, gave him two names, the first, Crimthan, meant a wolf, and the second, Colum, a dove. And these two words, curiously enough, summed up the whole character of the man; for all through his life he was brave and adventurous, all through his life there was a tenderness and peacefulness. Nor, surely, is it mere coincidence that the Hebrew word for dove is "Iona" and the Latin word for dove is "Columba". But in his earlier days, there was more of a warrior and a fighter about him, even though his friends knew him as "Colum of the Church". And still today the meaning of his name in Gaelic is "Colum of the Church".

This young prince was always a hard worker. He wasn't afraid to roll up his sleeves and take his share in the work, and on his holidays he would go away to some quiet place and there in the best way recreate or re-create himself, reading the old poetic tales of his race, "restoring his soul" by the green pastures and still waters, and then off to these other duties again.

Why he left Ireland is difficult to say for certain. There are many legends as to why; but we know *his* reason, for he told us himself, was that he "desired to go on a pilgrimage for Christ". He had learnt by making mistakes, because he was a wise man; and so he came from the land he loved to the land he was soon to love to spread the story of

Christ and unite the quarrelling tribes, "desiring to go on a pilgrimage for Christ".

With twelve men he crossed in small boats called coracles and landed on Iona, the Holy Isle, where the Druids had offered sacrifices to the unknown God; and there he made his headquarters, there he raised the standard to the only known God. From there he would set out with Iona as his base to preach "Him whom they ignorantly worshipped". He and his men built huts and chapels for daily service; he inscribed illuminated manuscripts and taught men not only what today we call theology, but also medicine, agriculture and astronomy. His followers were to be as good sailors in the sea as they were to be soldiers of the Lord, for their pilgrimage was to take them ever far by land and sea. And so they had to work hard on the land and they had to be able to build, not only places to live in, but boats. They were not only to be fishers of men but they were to fish for their food. They had to make their own clothes – in short, they had to be self-supporting. Columba and his men lived there happily together, for theirs was a happy faith, as the Christian faith truly lived must always be. Theirs was a humble faith – that too the Christian faith must always be. And there too, like true Christians, the little task was as great as the big. Above all, they were kind, not only to their fellow men but to strangers and to animals. And all men, be they king or beggar, were made welcome. From that island he set out to convert the savage tribes of Scotland – indeed, he claimed to have seen the Loch Ness monster when he was going up to convert the savage King Brude. At last when he died after blessing the Island and returning to his cell, working to the end in transcribing the psalms, he died with the words on his lips: "They that seek the Lord shall want no manner of thing that is good."

He was kind and children loved him. He was gentle, because animals of all sorts found him their friend and trusted him. Yet he was no stained-glass saint; there's nothing soft about him. Here's what one of his friends said: "He was tall and active, able to do and to endure; skilful with his pen, as well as with sail and oar; every day he spent some time in prayer, in reading, in writing, and in some hard manual work. He sang gloriously and was fond of Gaelic songs, and the music of the harp. Everybody loved him, and his face was radiant with cheerfulness." Can you imagine any better epitaph than that?

But never forget that he had his difficulties too, and they were very like yours and mine (most people's difficulties are very like yours and mine). But he mastered them, as you and I can master them too, as so many have done before and since his day. Though our circumstances may be very different, the way is very much the same.

St. Cuthbert
(635–687)

There are no places that I love more than the Lothians and the Borders and few places more than the Lammermuir Hills — these friendly hills that are green to the top. It is about a Lowland Scot that I want to speak to you for a minute or two now — a Lowland Scot who loved those green hills too. As a boy he was a shepherd on these hills and some of my Boys' Club must sometimes have slept near where long years ago he too must have slept, when they have gone out on expeditions for the Duke of Edinburgh Award and when he tended his sheep. They are comfortable hills to sleep on, for I have — many years ago now — slept on them myself — of course in summer time and on the heather; but this shepherd boy must have slept on them in all weathers and not always with the carefree mind of the walker or the camper.

The boy's name was Cuthbert, an orphan whom in his younger days a kindly widow looked after; he was always fit and full of life and fun, could outjump, outwrestle, outrun the boys around him; and they liked him and respected him and looked to him as their leader.

One day when he was on the hills with his sheep — he'd be about fifteen at the time — he saw a star falling from the sky (it was probably a shooting-star); and when shortly afterwards he heard that the great Bishop Aidan had died that night he thought it was a special message to him. He set out for Melrose and went straight to the Monastery there and asked to be taken in and join the brothers. (I remember most vividly as a boy seeing a shooting-star from my nursery window and my rather superstitious nurse telling us that that meant a good man had died that night; and next morning I heard my father tell my

mother that the great Alexander Whyte had died, and quietly to myself put two and two together!)

Well, when this fresh, fit, bright young boy arrived at the monastery there must have been something about him that immediately
struck the Prior for he turned to one of the monks and said, "Behold,
a servant of the Lord". He soon became one of the most outstanding
of the brothers, outstanding in all he did and loved by them all.
Trained in the hills, he used to go long journeys walking over the
much-loved Lowland hills, preaching the word of God and adminis-
tering the sacraments, a shepherd still though now with human sheep;
and at night he would rest again by the still green pastures and still
waters with the Good Shepherd beside him.

Then later he went to the Abbey founded by St. Aidan on Holy
Island off the Northumbrian coast where, as Prior of Lindisfarne, he
stayed for twelve years; a difficult period for the Abbey which he
made easy by his kindly tact and graciousness.

He built a little house on Farne Island – just opposite Bamburgh
and there for a number of years he stayed, refusing all honours, travel-
ling over the country as far as Carlisle, until at last the King persuaded
him in person to become Bishop of Lindisfarne. But though he still
had the heart and spirit of the young shepherd he was getting an old
man now, and knew he would soon die, and so he went back after
being only two years Bishop and died in his hermit's cell in 687. His
body was taken to be buried at Lindisfarne; but it now lies in Durham
Cathedral where two hundred years later it had to be removed because of the Danish invasion on the coast. There are many churches
called after him, including, of course, one of our greatest Edinburgh
churches. And on 20th March the Christian Church specially remembers him – St Cuthbert's Day.

And I'd like you to remember now something that Bede said
about him: "Such things that he taught other folk to do he first in his
own doing gave example of the same." This Lowland Scot who loved
the green hills, loved the beasts and the birds and all God's children;
for prayer to him was as much doing as saying. In these hectic rushing
days we have much to learn from the patience and serenity of St.
Cuthbert; and that is why I want you to remember him.

St. Francis Xavier
(1506–1552)

Among the many interesting people I met on the ship on a journey out to the Middle East were the dining-room waiters. They were always so courteous, so friendly, so cheerful, and so spotlessly clean with their white jackets, polished faces, and well-brushed hair. They were, moreover, what is known as 'coloured' people – no inappropriate name, for beside them most of us seemed in more senses than one quite colourless! I found that they came from Goa in India, and that they were Christians and good practising Roman Catholics. What a wonderful job they made of their quarters when they turned it into a chapel on Christmas Eve for their Christmas Mass. I remember how pleased and excited the Roman Catholic naval padre was when he took me to see it. Although they had to work very long hours each day, they still had found time to transform a part of the ship into something quite exceptional to make it more worthy of the worship they were to give to God at their Mass this Christmas Eve.

I asked the naval padre how it came about that all these men were Christians. And he told me that they were descendants of the men and women of Goa who away back in the middle of the sixteenth century had been won over to the Christian faith by St. Francis Xavier.

St. Francis Xavier – surely the most admired and loved of all the saints after his namesake of Assisi since the days of the apostles. Here is a man for you – a real man.

Francis Xavier surely sacrificed more than almost any other man for the sake of his fellow men . . . not merely did more, but in the most tryingly difficult circumstances. His terrific faith and his love for folk to win for them that faith, and the comfort of a few really grand friends kept him going. There were many in his own day thought that he was a failure. He received little or no encouragement – in fact, sometimes direct opposition – from people who ought to have known better – partly because of their jealousy, partly because of their worldly ambition – two of the foulest besetting sins as common today as then. In spite of that, and in spite of his own poor estimation of himself, except as a channel that God could use (which is really the only estimation that any man ought to have of himself) he went on, however thwarted, never giving in and never in his own estimation "getting there".

Whenever he really began to get down to some constructive work he was snatched away from it. But for Francis, every change, however sorry he was to leave, presented a new opportunity and he made the best of it.

And so he came to Goa, the home of these boys who waited on us on the ship; and there he rolled up his sleeves and got down – and sometimes on his knees – to clean up what was then one of the foulest cities in the East. It was a hard job, made harder by all he'd loved and left behind. When Francis was to return after a two years' visit to Japan he found that most of what he had built up had begun to fall down. So he just started again; but before much could be done he was sent to China and died, sick and almost alone, before he got there. His life – like our Lord, his Master's – had seemed a great failure. His "failures" had made him great, for he had never given in; nor had he ever turned the blame on to others, as we so often do, but on himself. As one of his biographers[6] has pointed out Francis was great, not so much because of what he did, as what he failed to do. And he is still remembered and loved, and nowhere more than in South India, as I was to find out years later when I visited these parts.

So that Christmas Eve I remembered him too; and thought that one day I must tell you about him. I saw his spirt still in these cheery clean young Goanese waiters, and most of all in their loyalty and love to our Lord whom they'd never have known had it not been for Francis.

And so I thought of all the failures we make of our lives (real failures) and how if we still try to carry on as best we can in the way we feel God wants, who knows but that even through us – through you and me – some good may come, though we may never live to see it?

[6] ARCHBISHOP ALSAN GOODIER, S.J. "There is a greater greatness than the greatness of success; and that is the greatness of failure. For that is the greatness of being, without the encouragement of doing; the greatness of sacrifice, of which others less great may reap the fruits."

Seven Lives

The seven lives I have chosen are of some people who are not as well-known as they ought to be; yet they, in their own different ways, influenced for good much in this country. They were all broadcast, either on the Ten to Eight Morning Service or in a series that I called Beacons to a Boy. *Some were printed in a booklet called* Great Men *and others under the title* They Looked Unto Him. *Each went quickly out of print. Though the former was reprinted in the U.S.A. in 1970, it is not obtainable in this country.*

The talk on Donald Hankey is based on the Introduction I wrote to a book which I edited with notes, published by Geoffrey Bles with a Foreword by Field Marshal Sir James Cassels, called The Beloved Captain.

Edward King
(1829–1910)

It was the beloved Canon Scott Holland of Christ Church, Oxford, who said that Edward King, Bishop of Lincoln, had just the sort of face you felt a human being ought to have. It was a face that shone with love; yet because of his loving-kindness his face could, too be stern. "Those kindly eyes", Scott Holland said, "could shine with a glint of steel, and the level brows, with their bushy eyebrows, could wear a look of sternness." For to those who love God and their fellows most, true kindness and true love must, with all its cheerfulness, show, if need be, a sternness equal with others as with himself. God's servants in this world are not here to be popular, or even to be liked; they are here to do God's work; and it is one of these glorious paradoxes of God that in the end of the day they are loved. Our Lord didn't seek popularity; He went about doing good, and not everyone liked it; and with the same hand that healed the sick he bore the whip of cords; and into the same hands with which he had blessed little children were hammered the nails of crucifixion. And now in His name, hands are stretched out to help the sick, or use the whip against evil things, or bless all God's children; or pierced and bleeding, receive the adoration of the world.

Edward King was one who ever believed that God stood by his side.

Bishop King himself once told how one day when visiting a man in gaol who had been sent there for robbery with violence he was surprised to hear the man say that once he had nearly killed him. And the old Bishop, with a smile, asked him to tell him more about it. "Well," said the convict, "it was this way – some pals and I, knowing that you used to go at a certain time each week to visit a sick man near Lincoln, decided that we would wait for you one night and knock you on the

head and take your money. But, as we waited behind the bushes we
saw that you were not alone; you had a friend who walked by your
side and we were afraid to attack the two of you." "But," smiled the
Bishop, "I never walked with anyone on that road from the village, I
was always alone." "I tell you," said the prisoner, "I saw quite clearly
your companion and he was with you all the way right up to your
own door."

Whether it was in the little parish of Wheatley where he started
his ministry beloved by all but not least by the plough boys, or as
Principal of Cuddleston, where perhaps he did his greatest work,
gently leading the lives of future pastors of the church so that through
all their lives his influence never left them, or surrounded by hundreds
of students he taught as Professor of Pastoral Theology at Oxford, or
as the ever beloved and saintly Bishop of Lincoln and the living
symbol of a true Father in God, he was the type of Good Shepherd
that our Lord would like to see in all the servants of His Church.

But because a man is a good man he is not therefore a dull, stern
man, who is always saying "don't" and wants to knock the fun out of
everything. That is never true, and never *less* true than of Bishop King.
True goodness must always be infectious, and laughter and fun are
two of God's greatest gifts. Once a God-fearing old lady said that the
old Bishop was a "dear old gentleman, but a wee bit too cheerful for a
Gospel Minister". The fact is that those who are really doing God's
work (and these can never be prigs or hypocrites or humbugs) have
the only right to be cheerful; and the real ones always are.

Archbishop Lang told how, as a Fellow of All Souls, and still a
member of the Church of Scotland, he decided to give up his career in
Law and enter the Church of England ministry, and how he went, shy
and nervously, to Lincoln to be confirmed by Edward King. He had
written to this, as he called him, "most beautiful, sane and cheerful of
saints", and had arrived on the eve of his confirmation. There happened
to be a retreat of ordinands going on, and during a meal in silence
broken only by the voice of a reader, he took his place quietly and
nervously beside the Bishop feeling "like a fish out of water". "The
dear old Bishop", said Lord Lang afterwards, "seemed to sense my dis-
comfort of mind, and putting his hand on my thigh, whispered to me,
"They're not half as good as they look, and I'm the naughtiest of them
all!" And, when Principal, he sent a note once to a rather tiresome
student who was overdoing it a bit during Holy Week: "Dearest

man", he wrote, "do eat some breakfast and come down to the level of your affectionate E.K."

No wonder an Oxford student said, "Whenever I saw him in the pulpit I wanted to be good and I knew that I could be." For he showed us the love that draws men to Christ.

For he believed that a principal of the Incarnation was to attract men by the human side and lead them into divine, since the great God Himself "for us men and for our salvation" became Man.

In his study at Lincoln, beside the chair at the window looking across the lovely gardens, there always stood a large ostrich egg which, long years before, the blacksmith at Wheatley had given him, and beside it a perfectly square wooden box, the parting gift of the carpenter who had said as he gave it, "I know you'd like it sir, for it's the same on every side." With these strange souvenirs of old affection were three of the pivots on which his life was formed — a prayer desk, and over the prayer desk a crucifix, and, over that, one word in Greek — the word Toil. "This world is the place to make friendships," he said, "it is in the next that we shall really enjoy them." In the memorial statue to him in Lincoln Cathedral, in the south transept where he sits blessing all who pass, the young and the old the saint and the sinner, are carved the words, "Beloved let us love one another for love is of God and everyone that loveth is born of God and knoweth God." He looked unto Him and was lightened . . . and in that light may we see light.

Sitting in the October evening light as his window of his Christ Church study and talking to Canon H. F. B. Mackay, then a new student, and telling him of the dangers and temptations that would face him, about the evil among some of those whom he might meet, and the seriousness of it, he added, "Remember there is a good deal of good among them. It is all there, dear fellow, it is all there, closed up like a tight bud in early spring, only wanting some sunshine and some rain to unfold into the flowers."

Arthur Henry Stanton
(1839–1913)

Of all men whom I didn't know who lived within the first half of this century, I should most like to have known Arthur Stanton. Yet the strange thing is that I almost feel I have known him; for I have met many who were his friends, and in every case there was something about them that was "different" – something about them that was Stanton. Of course most of them, like my father, had known him in his older days, but in Arthur Stanton's case that made little difference; for as an old man who had been with him at Rugby and Oxford said, "I never knew anyone whose face at the close of his life was so little changed."

Certainly in his case, the "child was father of the man"; for at Rugby he distinguished himself in the only two ways that anyone can claim any ground for distinction – in character and individuality. As one of his schoolboy friends put it, "He was good, but not goody – always full of fun and good humour." And when at the end of his student days he chose to go to the most difficult curacy he could tackle – to Mackonochie at St. Alban's, Holborn – he was doing no more than his friends would have expected of him. It was his first charge and he was twenty-three years old. It became his only charge, for he remained there all the rest of his life: fifty years a curate and, because he had independent means, with an income of five shillings a year! The Bishop of London had said to him when he was leaving Cuddlestone: "You know if you go to St. Alban's, you can never expect church preferment" – and he neither expected it, nor wanted it, nor got it – though almost as he was dying he declined the offer from another Bishop of London of a Prebendary's stall at St. Paul's.

Shortly after his ordination, he wrote to his mother that the most real way of working in a large city parish was for a band of ministers to live together and give up their time and money, and even health and life, if need be, to work in "the most glorious work ever given to men – that of saving souls; working to displace vice by purity, hatred by love, despair by joy", working, as he put it "never alone, but with Jesus and knowing this". That great conception of the Christian ministry remained with him all through his life.

Though he was a great preacher, he never regarded preaching as the most important part of his work, and even went as far as to say that "people are never better for sermons — at least not often". Yet it would be quite impossible to gauge the full influence of his sermons; and the reason for their greatness was not only that he put the sermons into his heart, but also into his head and heart.

When people looked back on his life and said, "There can never be anyone like Fr. Stanton" they recalled many different aspects. A business man, for example, would think of him as the greatest preacher he had ever heard. Another would tell you that what most impressed him was his care and love for the boys in his parish; if a boy were said to be unmanageable he'd say, "Now that's just the sort of boy I want." He'd play cricket with them, take them out into the country, play rounders with them in his shirtsleeves in Hyde Park or sit with them at the pantomime, roaring with laughter. He was always doing little kindnesses which are remembered; saying little kind words which stick in people's minds, trying all round to make anyone — especially a boy — happy, if he did not look so.

The richest and the poorest equally sought his friendship and advice; but it was the poor, and mostly those he loved to call the "undeserving poor" who sought him most — and whom most he sought. He was the friend of sinners and many were kept from crime, or further crime, because — as they put it — "Dad would take it so to heart" — and how well they knew him for, indeed, he did take it all to heart!

It was said of St. Francis de Sales that the best way to win his friendship was to do him an injury; and there was something of Francis de Sales in Father Stanton. There was, for example, the time when Stanton thought it wise to refuse a shilling to a beggar. When the beggar said: "Come on, Dad, I was the chap who sneaked your watch," Father Stanton looked at him in silence for a minute and then said: "Well, I think that does deserve a bob; here you are." Such was ever his sympathy with the underdog; for, as he put it, "God remembereth that we are but dust and you can't expect dust to be up to the mark all the time!" Once on a Palm Sunday some of his very rough boys asked him if he'd come out with them on Bank Holiday Friday. He told them that he couldn't do that for it was Good Friday. "It's the day our dear Lord died for us," he told them. There was a pause. "Well, what would you like us to do on Friday?"

"I'd like," said Arthur Stanton, "I'd like you to come to church." So
they said they'd come if he'd give them a hot cross bun each. Well,
they all came, and he gave them two buns. He'd never seen them in
church before, and they looked so clean and tidy and they knelt down
to say their prayers, though he didn't know who had taught them.
They joined with all their hearts in the service, and when they came
to the verse of the hymn:

> "O, I will follow Thee
> Star of my soul,
> Through the deep shades of life
> On to the goal."

They sang the last line as "to the gaol"! "And," said Father Stanton
telling the story later, "upon my word, before the next Good Friday
every one of them had been in gaol!"

But with his great sympathy for those who so needed the helping
care of the Church, Arthur Stanton could be what we in Scotland call
"a bonny fechter". He was valiant for the truth in the teaching of the
Church of our Lord; and he fought anything that was done to lessen
or cheapen the faith as he saw it. He was an uncompromising high
churchman; he and his colleagues were spied on by those who fought
and condemned his so-called ritualism. All his life he fought for principles that he honestly believed were right and true and scriptural; and
the wounds he received during the first part of his ministry, he carried
with him to the end. Because of his "high churchmanship" he was
inhibited by the Chaplain-General from preaching to the troops who
loved him, and by the Bishops in one diocese after another. For the
last thirty-seven years of his life, he was reckoned as a power with
whom the rulers of Church and State had to reckon. And for these
thirty-seven years, St. Alban's, Holburn, was his only ministry. Yet he
never resented how others worshipped, or tried to interfere with
them, if they were sincere in their worship of our Lord. As he once
said to some young university students: "Now, my dear boys, some
of you I know are going to be priests. Now when you are priests,
teach your people to love the Lord Jesus. Don't teach them to be
Church of England: teach them to love the Lord Jesus." He wrote to
his sister in the midst of one of the fiercest battles that the Puritans
were waging against him: "I go to Shepperton to preach for a dear
old Evangelical Calvinist. I am sure we shall get on, as he loves Jesus."
Whatever denomination, "high" church or "low" – he called Moody

and Sankey "two godly men", and Pope Leo XIII "a man sent by God" — it was their love of Christ that mattered.

So through all his life he carried with him the three great gifts that St. Paul tells us are communicated by the laying on of hands — the gifts of power, love and a sound mind. And so for fifty years he remained a curate in a London church, loved and respected and sometimes feared for his passion for the truth — whatever the consequences.

He had no worldly ambitions; but there was one honour he was unable to refuse. He couldn't stop the people of London giving him a public funeral. Through crowded streets his body was borne in a great procession — borne by those who had served so long with him — now old, old men . . . and as they crossed the bridge on the Surrey shore the great crowds began to sing:

"The strife is o'er, the battle done . . . Alleluia."

Surely Arthur Stanton that day inherited eternal life; for as a young man with great possessions he had knelt at the feet of Jesus, whom, having sold all that he had and given to the poor, he followed. But perhaps it is best left to one of his own rough boys to sum up quite unconsciously the life and influence of Arthur Stanton. "Do you", asked a well-meaning court missionary to the boy, "do you know Jesus?" "No, sir," replied the boy, "but I know a friend of his who lives up our way — Father Stanton."

John S. Stansfield
(1854–1939)

Westminster Abbey; a new Bishop (C. S. Woodward) is to be consecrated; the large procession of choirboys, of Bishops and other clergy; the Archbishop of Canterbury slowly enters, as the organ peals out, and passes through the large congregation. Quietly, hardly noticed, there entered a white-haired Minister, with a trim white beard, who took his seat and knelt down to say his prayers. "Perhaps," thought a man who was present, "Perhaps no one besides 'Wooder' and myself realises that *that* is the greatest man under the roof of the Abbey today."

The man was Barclay Baron, and many today owe him a debt of real gratitude for bringing again to life "The Doctor."

William Temple has told how, during his second year at Oxford, he first met John Stansfield, "The Doctor", whom he later described as "one of the greatest men and truest Christians whom I have known". He was taken into a basement room where a crowd sat round the wall on benches. In the middle was the Doctor delivering a five minute sermon and behind stood Temple. Then he suddenly turned and got into a corner behind a screen where there was a table and three chairs. Temple sat on one, the Doctor on another, and each patient in turn on the third. "Put out your tongue", the Doctor would say. "Where did you go to Church last Sunday?" "Open your mouth" . . . "Why not?" "Say ninety-nine". "Well, I'll give you some medicine, but mind you say your prayers and go to church in future."

The doctor did all the speaking, the patient being usually in a position that made speech impossible. Then he turned to William Temple and said, "We must have finished the first lot by now and there will be another crowd; go out and speak the word to them for a few minutes." And so the nervous young student, later to become Archbishop both of Canterbury and York, went out and tried to remember bits of the sermon he had heard the day before in St. Paul's! But the doctor seemed pleased.

He was truly a remarkable man. Leaving school at fifteen, it wasn't until he was twenty-two that he settled in a job which he held for over thirty years in Customs and Excise; but hard though he worked at his job, he worked harder in his spare time, and when he was transferred to an Oxford branch he spent his spare time as an undergraduate at Exeter College, Oxford. He rose at five-thirty each day, worked at his books, went to his business and when evening came – back to his books again. He had set his mind on entering the church, but a long way lay ahead of him. He got his degree and then decided to become a doctor first, and when he was transferred for a time to Glasgow he carried on his studies at the Royal Infirmary there.

Back in London he was asked to found a small Medical Mission and so he came to what was at the time "the greatest area of unbroken poverty in England", Bermondsey. So began the Oxford Medical

Mission which became the justly famous Oxford and Bermondsey Club. Students and leaders – many later to become famous and who include in the church alone three Archbishops and thirteen Bishops – learnt what Barclay Baron so happily calls the "game" of leadership under his leading. He brought them with him to give; and they stayed to receive.

In part of his quarters he saw his patients, in part he had his boys' club; the students and leaders lived mostly with him in the same building later; the life was Spartan to a degree, the staple diet for a time bread and treacle. To his well-disciplined happy camp at Hordon boys without money would walk twenty-six miles. Combining the work of doctor and Club leader after thirty-three years of office routine he became a parson too. He went to Oxford, to Africa, to Spelsbury, but it is Bermondsey which remembers him most.

As a family of brothers he taught them, as he did himself, to do all to the glory or God. "A church is either on ice or on fire," said the Doctor and, "The Bible promises no loaves to the loafer." One of the most effective sermons he ever preached lasted fifteen seconds. After some of the roughs in the early days had defied a club leader and knocked the Club around a bit, the Doctor strode in unannounced to take the service. Everyone sat down, some nervously holding their hymn books; the Doctor stared at them, stared at the mess and preached his sermon: "Dear chaps, this room is disgustingly untidy, *disgustingly* untidy. We are going to clean it up together after prayers. And we are going to do it all for the Glory of God, for the Glory of God."

When Canon Stansfield died, an old man of 85, they held a Thanksgiving not a Memorial Service. And this was the closing prayer: "We thank Thee, Lord and Father, for sending to us someone who taught us what Jesus Christ was really like; he made the picture step out of the frame, and in trying to follow him, we tried to become better men. Please send us more like the Doctor, and so draw us a bit closer to Jesus Christ our Lord."

Donald W. A. Hankey
(1884–1916)

In my little cabin at our Boys' Club Camp which for forty years I had at Skateraw by the sea, you would find among my changing books a few that were always there – a New Testament, a Prayer Book, books on birds and flowers and animals, and with them a book called *A Student at Arms*. I suppose I could call it one of my "desert island" books. The author – Donald Hankey – was a man I'd like so much to have known: he really understood the ordinary man without condoning his faults; and he saw the goodness even in the worst and brought it out.

Donald W. Alers Hankey entered Rugby, the youngest of a family of seven, where three of his older brothers had been before him – Hugh, his great hero of his young days, so tragically killed at Paardeburg at the age of twenty-seven, Maurice, later the Right Hon. Lord Hankey, and Clement. He was born at Brighton in 1884 and in his Prep School already showed something of the stuff of which he was made. For example, his sister told how, on one occasion, he came back from school obviously very upset. They could get nothing out of him. At last he flared up. His face reddened, his eyes burned like coals; and, in a voice trembling with rage, he said, ". . . talks about things that I won't even think!"

He entered the sixth form at Rugby when he was sixteen and a half and, before he was seventeen, the Royal Military Academy, Woolwich, where he began to doubt both his liking and his fitness for the Army. He told his father that he thought he would like to enter the Church; but his father wisely advised him to wait for, as he put it, "a few years in the Army would be no bad training for a parson."

And so he was commissioned into the Royal Garrison Artillery and at the age of twenty was sent to the Island of Mauritius. He left there on medical advice, and a month after his return in November 1906 his father died. Soon after he resigned his commission and after a short visit to Italy he went up to Corpus Christi College, Oxford, in October of that year. The influence of the Rugby Mission at Notting Hill, and even greater the influence of meeting John Stansfield at

Bermondsey and the work he did for the Oxford and Bermondsey Boys' Club, fitted him more than anything else for the great days that were to lie ahead, all the greater because they were so few.

Of Dr. Stansfield and the Oxford and Bermondsey Club I have already written. It was into this atmosphere that Donald Hankey found himself plunged, and along with him there were some men who became some of the greatest leaders of our time.

As I mention later, when he first went to Bermondsey no one knew why he had come. He seemed to be a misfit. But soon those who had begun by ragging him were the first to confide in him; and they soon realised that "none understood them better than Donald". Like the others he became a resident there and while there wrote – largely as confirmation talks to the boys – *The Lord of All Good Life*.[1]

In order to try to bridge the gulf he felt between the Bermondsey life and his own, he travelled steerage to Australia dressed in old clothes: he thought too that he might be able to start a farm there for the London boys. After over a year he returned to Bermondsey.

Then the war came and he joined up at once in Kitchener's "First Hundred Thousand". The day after he enlisted in the Rifle Brigade he was made a Corporal and before the week was over he was a sergeant, with what ups and downs we shall see later. At length, and with reluctance, he was persuaded to take a commission and, though commissioned into the R.G.A. again, he asked and was granted a transfer into his brother Hugh's Regiment, the Royal Warwickshire.

It was while in the army that he wrote articles for The Spectator under the name of "A Student at Arms"; and in a short time every one was talking about this anonymous writer who knew so intimately the life and feeling of the citizen in uniform. The essays are as fresh today as the day they were written and are as applicable not only to the citizen or regular soldier, but to leadership in commerce and industry as well as to youth. His *A Book of Wisdom*, for instance, contains such sayings as "To know one's limitations is a mark of wisdom; to rest content with them merits contempt"; or "True religion is betting your life there is a God"; or "The disbeliever loses this world, and risks losing the next"; or that beatitude that was so soon to apply to himself, "Blessed is he of whom it has been said that he so loved giving that he even gave his own life."

Here are extracts from some of his greatest essays. Take, for

[1] For these days and much more see *The Doctor*, by Barclay Baron.

example, that fine passage where he describes the "lost sheep" in the
Kitchener Battalions – a passage which made the then Editor of The
Spectator say that "With all sincerity an author of today might parody
Wolfe and declare that he would rather have written that passage than
won a general action."

       They plunged head-long down the stony path of glory,
but in their haste they stumbled over every stone! And when
they did that, they put us all out of stride, so crowded was the
path. Were they promoted? They promptly celebrated the
fact in a fashion that secured their immediate reduction. Were
they reduced to the ranks? Then they were in hot water from
early morn to dewy eve, and such was their irrepressible
charm that hot water lost its terrors. To be a defaulter in such
a merry company was a privilege rather than a disgrace. So in
despair we promoted them again, hoping that by giving them
a little responsibility we should enlist them on the side of
good order and discipline. Vain hope! There are things that
cannot be overlooked even in a Kitchener Battalion.

   Yet, notice how these same lost sheep changed as they stood in the
hour that matched the test of battle:

       Then at last we got out. We were confronted with death,
danger and death. And then they came to their own. We
could no longer compete with them . . . Yet they who had
formerly been our despair were now our glory. Their spirits
effervesced. Their wit sparkled. Hunger and thirst could not
depress them. Rain could not damp them. Cold could not chill
them. Every hardship became a joke. They did not endure
hardship, they derided it . . . As for death, it was, in a way,
the greatest joke of all. In a way, for if it were another
fellow who was hit, it was an occasion for tenderness and
grief . . . With a gay heart they gave their greatest gift, and
with a smile to think that anything they had to give was of
value . . . They had been lost, but they found the path that led
them home; and when at last they laid their lives at the feet of
the Good Shepherd, what could they do but smile?

   You see what I mean; you see why that book was always in my
Cabin.

   The study I like best is the one of his captain – "The Beloved
Captain" he called him. It's one of the greatest pictures of leadership

that anyone could ever have; and I've read it so often that I know it nearly by heart:

> He came in the early days, when we were still at recruit drills under the hot September sun. Tall, erect, smiling; so we first saw him and so he remained till the end.

And his "end" came not so very long before Donald Hankey's; and it was because the Beloved Captain died before him that he found death more easy – so he told us. When the Captain was killed, he said:

> But he lives: somehow he lives. And we who knew him do not forget. We feel his eyes on us. We still work for that wonderful smile of his. There are not many of the old lot left now; but I think that those who went have seen him. When they got to the other side I think they were met. Some One said, "Well done, good and faithful servant." And as they knelt before that gracious pierced Figure, I reckon they saw nearby the Captain's smile. Anyway, in that faith let me die, if death should come my way; and so I think I shall die content.

Death came his way on the Somme in October 1916. Before the attack some who came through told how he knelt with his men in prayer. And then shortly he told them what lay before them; "If wounded, Blighty; if killed, the Resurrection." Then over the top they went, and he was last seen rallying his men. That night he was found close to the trench, the winning of which had cost him his life.

But his message and his spirit still lives for these days. He has shown us that, given the right leaders and leadership in all forms of life, we can all find what John Buchan once expressed so well, when writing of his hero Montrose, "There is in all men, even the basest, some kinship with the Divine, something which is capable of rising superior to common passions and the lure of easy reward, superior to pain and loss, superior even to death. The true leader evokes this . . . The task of leadership is not to put greatness into humanity, but to elicit it, for the greatness is there already."

Sir Alexander Paterson
(1884–1947)

"Across the Bridges." I suppose there can be no better way of introducing Sir Alexander Paterson than with these three words. They are not only the title of the one book he wrote – a quite unpretentious volume which has had at the time a quite tremendous influence – but they would seem to sum up the whole of his life's work. An outstretched hand of friendship is no bridge unless there is a hand to grasp it. But when Alec Paterson stretched out his hand only a bridge could follow it.

Alec Paterson was the leader of a very small but remarkable group at the beginning of this century to which, later, others became attached. It was a group of men whose true greatness was partly to be found in their almost deliberate obscurity; ony the inner circle know how much they have given to the world at large. Barclay Baron, Donald Hankey, Roland Phillips, Stanley Nairne, F. M. Crum, "Nunky" Brown for example with Alec Paterson himself as the king of them all, are known and loved in the wide yet reserved world of Boys' Clubs, and Toc H. and Social Reform. Yet even among those who most benefited by them, so often their names are but names: and that I submit surely is part of their greatness. Not one of them sought fame, but all of them earned it; none sought riches, but how great are the riches they have bestowed on the world! They did not *talk* about fellowship and service: they served their fellows without hope or desire of reward – except the only reward really worth having – that of knowing that they did God's will. They served their fellows without fear of the consequences, except that some place or something or some person – yes, above all, and far above all, some person – was the better for it.

From the inspiration and direction of this group, led by Alec Paterson, came so much of all that is good in the Boys' Clubs as we know them today. From Alec Paterson and his contemporaries came so much of the consolidation of Toc H., of work to care for the underprivileged, of concern for the boy who got into trouble, of reform for such boys in borstal or prison. Striving to give to all men and women a chance, they equally stand as the Apostles of the second chance.

Their very humility in all they did makes it hard to give details of the way they did it.

I have taken Alec Paterson as an example because, as I have said, he was the acknowledged leader of them all. Beginning his great work of leadership at Oxford when he first went up as an undergraduate at the age of eighteen, he never left it all his life. Though he was honoured by the King and by the Government and, for him probably most of all by those to whom he had given a second chance, the honour that would most have pleased him (though it would greatly have embarrassed him) would be to know – as somehow surely he does know – that amidst the Bermondsey he so loved and which was so much destroyed in the last war, there is a square symbolizing the new Bermondsey. This square most appropriately bears the name of him who often dreamed of the thought of a new Bermondsey – Paterson Square.

At Oxford he was able to persuade the Senior Proctor to allow him – as a very special concession – to visit the places where conditions were at their worst. And he and one or two others, including Barclay Baron, who was probably the greatest friend that Alec Paterson had throughout the rest of his life, used to spend some evenings each week with the down-and-outs, play dominoes with them, share the common cup, or rather perhaps basin, of tea, trying by his friendship to make them better fellows. Though perhaps in these earlier days the successes were hardly great, he at least was going through a good school of apprenticeship for the task which lay before him throughout the rest of his life.

The first bridge he made was the bridge between the Oxford student and the down-and-out – not a very easy bridge and not one that was safe for many to cross, but at least a beginning for the many other bridges he was to build. When he left Oxford he left without very much academic distinction, though later his College was to make him an Honorary Fellow, and yet he was probably one of the two great personalities of his time at University, the other being William Temple. Though I like to think that while at Oxford he heard Arthur Stanton speak to the students on one of his rare but rewarding visits, probably one could give credit most of all in these days to a man universally known and loved and respected as "The Doctor" – John Stanfield, who as I have already mentioned, was regarded by Archbishop Temple as one of the greatest men and truest Christians he had ever known. For it was John Stansfield who persuaded Alec Paterson and five others to help at Bermondsey – "just for a fortnight" – on their first holiday. "Just for a fortnight" became twenty-one years; and the Oxford Medical Mission became the more famous Oxford and Bermondsey Club. Once again it was Alec Paterson who became the leader – though he was the last to realise it. He wasn't concerned with position in life, indeed he called himself the "Junior Resident".

His great work with the Boys' Clubs was enhanced by the fact that he lived among the people, on the top of a noisy tenement in a room which was distinctive from the others round it only because it had a bath in it, and because the walls were covered with photographs of his many friends, as well as a list of the names of forty ragged and noisy small boys whom he was now teaching in an elementary school at Bermondsey, a list headed "Of such is the Kingdom of Heaven". It was here that he wrote *Across the Bridges*, that book still regarded as a landmark.

In this tenement room the neighbours knew him as a friend. To half their children he was a godfather. He was their unofficial lawyer, he was their "lay priest", as Donald Hankey once called him. It was about this time that the Children's Charter was being drafted by Lord Samuel, the Charter that later became known as the Children's Act, 1908. And it was this man who knew so much about boys, who was living unobtrusively in this over-crowded and noisy section of London, that Lord Samuel sent for at the Home Office. And it was this unknown man who was to add thirty amendments to the Bill.

In 1910 Winston Churchill, then Home Secretary, gave Alec Paterson his first appointment that was to become later his life-work and to make prisoners ever stand in his debt – a life-work that aimed to turn into the world better men than they had been when they went to prison, freed from an old stigma as filled with new spirt. It was through Churchill that Alec Paterson began the work of interviewing those who had been convicts and trying to resettle them in life, and later trying to interest many other people in prison work, not least through Toc H. of which he had now become Chairman. For it was along with "Tubby" Clayton and Dick Sheppard that he produced the four points of the Toc H. compass: to love widely, to build bravely, to think fairly, and witness humbly – four points, if you come to think of it, which do much to sum up the whole Christian faith and would do almost anything to create peace in the world.

SIR ALEXANDER PATERSON 41

To the end of his days Paterson loved Toc H., though his many other commitments prevented him from doing as much as he would have liked latterly to do. At the Birthday Festival of Toc H. in 1922 when the lamps were lit for the first time by the Prince of Wales, he said: "Ours is a task that knows no limits. It is not and easy task, but it is not beyond our endurance. There can be no true comradeship without surrender, no true service without sacrifice. We hope to carry on a holy and ceaseless war against pride and snobbery and content wherever we meet them . . . In spirit of Jesus Christ we are joined together, and we shall go forward, setting our course always not by the waves but by the stars."

He has his greatest memorials in the lives of men to whom he gave the second chance. He has a memorial, too, in the Children's Act of 1908, which I have mentioned; and even more in the Criminal Justice Bill of 1947 which was placed on the Statute Book three weeks after his death – a memorial which the then Home Secretary, Chuter Ede, acknowledged when he said that, during the past thirty yearts or so, very great reforms had been carried out and he regretted very much that one of the men who had undoubtedly given a lead – not merely to this country but to many other countries – on the subject of penal reform had passed away just before the Bill came before the House. Even though the "Junior Resident" never wanted praise or credit, it was a kind thing to say, and he always loved kindness: it was a true thing to say, and he was always valiant for truth.

Barclay Baron, who as I have said, was probably his best friend, tells how he said goodbye to him. "On a November evening last year, in Alec's little house in Chelsea, I left his wife and daughter for a while and was alone with him upstairs. I knew this was goodbye. He was breathing quietly in the sleep from which he would not awake. Already he was in sight of the last Bridge, which each one of us must sooner or later cross alone to the other side. It seemed the trumpets were sounding to welcome a servant of the King of that Country where new tasks are given to those who kept faith with Him."

As we remember Alec Paterson, let us remember his words: "Ours is a task that knows no limits. It is not an easy task, but it is not beyond our endurance. There can be no true comradeship without surrender, no true service without sacrifice. We hope to carry on a holy and ceaseless war against pride and snobbery and content wherever we meet them . . . In the spirit of Jesus Christ we are joined

together, and we shall go forward, setting our course always not by
the waves but by the stars."

Kingsley Ogilvie Fairbridge
(1885–1934)

"I camped with strange men at night and heard strange speech and
tales . . . a lad of thirteen dressed in knicker-bockers and shirtsleeves,
I walked on the outskirts of the Empire". . . . Or here as a boy of
twelve, trying to catch up on his father. "For the next thirty, forty –
or as I thought fifty miles I would tramp westwards, never seeing a
white man, but following winding paths that led amongst the hills . . .
At any turn of the path I might come face to face with a lion, and
then I would have to kneel and shoot straight – my life depending on
it. Or I might walk right into a herd of elephants. Worse still, a leopard
might leap our frail skerm at night."

By the time he was fifteen, Kingsley Ogilvie Fairbridge had done
more pioneering, run more risks, faced more dangers, and proved
himself more of a man than most people are able to do throughout
their lives. Yet all the while this young boy, even at that age, had a
vision. A chance adventure came at the age of twelve when, driven by
"pride and hunger", as he tells us, he found a task and dreamed a
dream which held him all the days of his boyhood and occupied him
every working hour and which would never be fulfilled even though,
as he put it, he lived till he was over eighty.

"And so," he wrote, remembering an adventure that he had had
as a boy of thirteen, "I went ahead on the tide of progress wondering
and observing and thinking of the thousands of homesteads that
would some day dot these fields."

At sixteen he travelled to England all by himself, arriving one
Sunday morning with hardly a penny in his pockets into a seemingly
empty London, for he had even forgotten the address of his grand-
mother who lived there. But largely possibly due to trophies he wore on
his hat because, like a boy he liked to wear badges, the kind London

people took an interest in him. But when he returned to Rhodesia a year later it was not the great sights that remained in his memory, but the sights of neglected children in poor surroundings. It was these children with so little chance that most weighed with him on his return. During the next three years in the wild places he lived, he still thought about them.

What a grand thing it would be, he thought, if these young children could get the same open-air chance as he had! What a grand thing it would be to make them into good farmers. And so at the age of twenty his early vision became his purpose in life. The father whom he had always trusted was taken into his confidence; and the father told him that it would take some time and he would not get much thanks for it, but bade him God-speed. And so he became at the age of twenty-one a Rhodes scholar at Oxford University. He who had left school at eleven, fought exams as hard as he'd fought anything, and never allowing his failings to get him down, he won. When he was at Oxford he realised that he must, if he was to do anything, win people's respect. He did this by the greatness of his character; but he also determined to win a blue, and he chose boxing.

Although at first he was beaten by Julian Grenfell, he put up a great fight; but far more important than that, he won the friendship of Grenfell. And the following year he was even to beat him and so win his coveted blue. All the time his one aim in life never left him. Any credit he won, any praise that came to him, was all for "the Cause". One of his most difficult tasks was to learn how to make a speech and he did this, pleading for the boys who ought to have a chance; and again, not without a tussle, he won through.

By 1912 he had gone out to Australia with his wife and started the famous Fairbridge Schools. But once again he was to meet with difficulties. The First World War came; support at home was almost impossible and all he could do was to go back and stir up fresh interest. The real difficulty would be to keep the Farm going without any funds – for when all was said and done, there was not much use appealing for something that had ceased to exist! Then came that meeting with the boys which shows how great a leader was Fairbridge. He gathered all of them together to say goodbye to them. The boys were restless and rather more excited than usual. One could feel a sense of mystery – there was a secret somewhere. And then came shyly and delightedly a presentation for Kingsley Fairbridge's wife and then a

suitcase for himself – a presentation which must have been hard to get
for it meant many weeks working and saving. One could imagine
how moved Kingsley Fairbridge must have been with them . . . He
talks to them, and like a true leader takes them into his confidence. He
tells them about his great vision – the vision that had come first to
him as a boy: a magnificent farm where everyone is happy with both
boys and girls and then when that was finished, more and more farms
all over the Empire! He tells of his going home to try and raise funds
and how he wants to take more boys and more girls away from the
conditions they so often have to live in, and give them a chance. They
too, he tells them, will learn the great art of playing games and enjoy-
ing them whether they win or lose. And then he tells them how the
Farm must go on even though he has not got the money to keep it
going. The staff, he tells them are going to stay on and then comes the
great challenge. He looks at them intently, yes, lovingly.

"I want", he says, "I want six boys to remain and be the School."
There was a pause. The boys were getting restive again, and then he
goes on: "All of you are now old enough and capable enough to go
out and earn your own living. You can easily find places from the
many farmers wanting boys. You will begin with 10s. a week and
your food. Soon, if you do well, you will earn fifteen shillings, twenty
shillings and perhaps thirty shillings a week. If you stay here I can only
offer you five shillings. That means a big sacrifice if you decide to stay
on."

He pauses again, he looks at them, the room is all astir and
Fairbridge holds up his hand. "I want you to be quite clear", he said,
"that it is all quite uncertain. I may fail, some say I will fail. That
would be the end of the Farm. Then you would have wasted eight or
nine months, and I can quite understand how you – the older boys
especially – are keen to start on your own. On the other hand, it may
mean that by staying on here and keeping the flag flying you will
have saved the life of the Farm School. But you must remember it is
going to be very dull for you; no excitement, no honour or glory, just
the usual work and more responsibility. Consider it, boys." Fairbridge
looks at them. Not a sound. "Now boys, who will volunteer? Think
well." There is no hesitation – every hand shoots up in the air!

He returned after the war with £30,000, a large sum in those days,
and new recruits, and happily he was able to see his vision come true.
He was only thirty-nine when he died in 1924. But who can deny that

he left a challenge not only to help the Fairbridge Schools but to help thousands of ordinary folk in their ordinary every-day life . . . a life which demands a tremendous loyalty of each one of us? — "even though it is going to be very dull sometimes", and there is "no excitement and no honour or glory, just the usual work and quite a bit of responsibility."

'X'[2]

Now that I come to think of it, I don't even remember his name. You see, at that time — "Invasion Time, 1940" — we met so many people and for so short a time. It is quite impossible to remember names; or, for that matter, anything at all about them. As a padre, I had more opportunity for meeting people than most; and of course, it was a part of my job. We were a Scottish Division in Norfolk and the surrounding counties, and it was part of the padre's job to get to know the local people and let them see we Scots were a friendly crowd of chaps, as well as to see to it that they became a friendly crowd to us. I would say — after a polite opening — " . . . and if you have any spare vegetables or strawberries or apples, I'd be very glad to take them off your hands for the men up the road", and " . . . we're rather short of books at the moment — you see, we lost everything in France in June, and if you have any spare books we would be very pleased to have them" . . . and so on. And I'd return to the unit with my "kill" in the little car I had, with the ever faithful "Mac" at the wheel: but to you please, L/Cpl. Walter MacLean of Musselburgh, and later Sgt. MacLean in India. It was on one of these expeditions (which I made usually about twice a week) that I met him, the man whose name I cannot recall . . .

He lived in a quaint and lovely old house covered in climbing roses and clematis and honeysuckle; and as I stepped out of the car into the bright sunshine of his courtyard, the air was rich with the scent of flowers and the hum of bees and the song of the birds — and

[2] I wish I could remember his name. But it doesn't really matter . . . to me he will always be unforgettable — one of the most unforgettable men I have ever met.

the war seemed very far away, the thought of invasion a distant
dream. This was peace.

I didn't need to ring the bell, for he came to the door to meet me.
He had a sunburnt, wrinkled face, a kind and cheerful face. He had
white hair and bushy eyebrows and clear, blue eyes that spoke kindness before his lips moved. In one hand he carried a straw garden hat
and in the other a wicker basket; but he quickly put them down and
asked me to come in without ever asking why I had come, and led me
to the sitting room and left me there for a minute.

"I won't be a minute," he said, "there's a lovely view from the
window and there's the "Field" to look at."

It was a lovely view, and a lovely room to view it from – old
oak furniture and fine old prints on the wall, and above the fireplace
a photo – rather faded – of a young girl of about seventeen – his
daughter I presumed. I didn't want to look at the "Field" – there was
so much else to look at. In any case, he came back in a few minutes.
He didn't say much; he lit his pipe and so I lit mine; I wasn't quite
sure how to begin. And then I said: "That's a very lovely picture
there, sir. Is that your daughter?"

The old man smiled – "Oh no", he said, "that's my wife; and it's
so like her. You'll see for yourself how like her it is; she'll be here
in a minute – but come along in to my study. Just a minute, let me
show you the view first . . ." Then I heard the distant clink of cups,
and the door opened and in came a beautiful old lady carrying a tray.
"Here is my wife," he said, "I said you'd see her in a minute."

I shook hands with her. "You'll have a cup of tea, won't you?"
she asked, "It's so refreshing in this warm weather."

Quietly I looked at the photograph. No, it couldn't be the same.
It is "so like her" he'd said. And then it dawned on me that the old
man still saw the young girl of seventeen where I saw a dear old lady.
They had been married for fifty years. "It's so like her," he said,
"you'll see her in minute . . ."

His study was what, by this time, I'd imagined it would be; in fact
it was all that a dream study should be. Shelves of books looked kindly
down like rows of friends; and as though they were not enough, portraits and pictures of other friends filled up the remaining gaps in the
walls. He was talking more now; not at first about himself and his
his house, but about the soldiers who had come to stay as welcome
neighbours. I did not need to ask him for anything; he offered more

than I had dared to ask — not only fruit and books, but hot baths and the hospitality of his garden and his house. And as he talked I learnt more about him. He was the parson and the squire; for over two hundred years this house and the old church beside it had been handed down from father to son.

Then I noticed the portrait: a magnificent picture in oils of a fine-looking man in a black gown and an Oxford hood. It wasn't just the good painting that held my attention; it was the strange feeling that I had seen it somewhere before reproduced in a book. I was trying to remember where, and then it dawned on me. "I hope you won't think me very inquisitive, sir," I said, "but that portrait there, is that the Dr. Arnold of Rugby?" For that's who I thought it was — Arnold, the hero of Tom Brown's Schooldays, Arnold the greatest headmaster of the last century about whom the boys at Rugby said: "You can never tell old Arnold a lie, because he always believes a fellow." And the old man looked up and smiled.

"No," he replied slowly, and his eyes twinkled even more than before; "No, it's not Dr. Arnold. But you couldn't have said a happier or nicer thing. That is the portrait of my father when he was a young man. It's a good picture; it was exhibited many years ago in the Royal Academy, and it has been here ever since. How pleased my father would have been to hear you say that, though; for he was in Dr. Arnold's form at Rugby and he just worshipped his great headmaster. There, over there, is a print of Dr. Arnold . . . come to think of it, they are rather alike. Oh, he would have been pleased to hear you say that."

And then I remembered how it was said that boys who left Dr. Arnold's form at Rugby School left stamped in the image of their great headmaster. "That must have been like the disciples," added the old man, "you remember how they took knowledge of them that they had been with Jesus."

I heard later that the old man was dead and his ever-young wife had died very shortly afterwards. A fellow who had gone back there to marry one of the local girls told me that the manor house and the church had, after two hundred years, passed into different hands. The folk around his countryside will never forget him. And I shall never forget him either. I wish I could remember his name. But it doesn't really matter. To me shall always be unforgettable.

Seven Early Morning Talks

These talks were given in what used to be called "Lift up your Hearts" on the B.B.C. National programme. They are taken from two booklets published at the kind request of so many listeners — Roses in December and Haply I May Remember — and quickly went out of print. I have here selected seven of the talks that were given at these times.

The Things that Really Matter

Although I have been in the same Church all my Ministry, I have moved my Manse four times. The first Manse was built about the time that Bonnie Prince Charlie came to Edinburgh; but it was shortly afterwards condemned and is now part of the site of the Moray House College of Education Swimming Pool.

Then I moved into Acheson House, built in 1633, opposite my Church – now the Scottish Craft Centre. I then went to a Regency house overlooking the parish. But I always had the intention that one day the Manse would again be not merely in the centre of the parish, but one particular centre on which I had had my eyes for quite a long time – the old Manse of Canongate which had been built in 1690 and was last used by one of my predecessors in 1832. Well, after long negotiations, and a complete work of restoration, I got back into that old house in 1957.

Now each of these moves meant taking with me all kinds of things I thought I couldn't do without; and, how things collect in a house when you've been living in it for a while – papers, pictures, and books. I determined this time to be quite ruthless and take with me only the things I really needed. But how hard it was to choose *what* I really needed. I determined, for example, that I must destroy some old letters and photographs; and then I found I couldn't really throw that one out, or this one here. They all brought back too many memories – groups, and souvenirs and all the rest of it. There they were at the top of the former house, and there they are at the top of my house still. I remember Don Bernard Clements (who I always thought was the best broadcaster that ever came over the B.B.C.) telling me that when he left to go to All Saints', Margaret Street, he put all kinds of things that he felt he would need in cases, and though he had been there for quite a long time he had never looked at one of them.

If you come to think about it, what a lot of useless stuff we do carry about with us. I look back on the days of war and remember how small were the possessions we could take with us; and, on the whole, how adequate they were for our needs. After all, we brought nothing into this world and it's perfectly certain we'll take nothing out of it – there are no pockets in a shroud! Someone once said that a man should live so that if he was shipwrecked he would still carry on him his greatest possessions. All of us are resident aliens on this earth and the only permanent possessions we have are our immortal souls; and yet how often do we forget that, and regard as of least importance the most important part of us? One of my letters that I treasure most is from the late Mgr. Ronald Knox in which he wrote to me, knowing he was very soon to die, – "The nearer approach of death drives me back more than ever to the formula, 'Nothing in my hand I bring', really nothing." You may remember the story of a man in the Bible who gathered all he had into barns and said to his soul that he needn't bother because now he had all he waned; and how that very night his soul was required of him.

I don't mean we shouldn't make provision for tomorrow for the sake of our loved ones, and those who are dependent on us, but I do mean that we shouldn't consider so much our own selfish interests. John Quincy Adams, the great American President, when he was asked on his eightieth birthday how he was, said, "I thank you John Quincy Adams is well, but the house in which he lives at present is becoming dilapidated . . . I think John Quincy Adams will have to move out of it soon. But he himself is quite well."

As a traveller and not a permanent resident in the world may I leave you with this thought – "What is it that really matters most to you – that is really worth keeping?"

God bless you and all whom you love, wherever they may be.

Roses in December

There was not much of a garden when I came into my present Manse. It had not been used as a garden for over one hundred years; but it

soon began to look better. It took time of course; and now, with the
various shrubs we planted growing up, my grand-nieces call it "the
secret garden".

A garden is such a thrilling thing. First the seed, and then the
coming up, and then the flower; and you get the feeling that though
you haven't made a single thing you have at least done something for
which you begin to see results. You have made the place just a little
bit lovelier than it would have been if you had not been there. And
your life and mine should be like that. Wherever our lot is cast, in
perhaps some quite small and insignificant place, we can leave it even
a *little* better just because, well, just because we have been there. And
perhaps, like that tree we put in which will continue to grow long
after we have gone, we can leave something after we have gone too.

Of the flowers in the garden those I love best are roses. I love their
form, and their colour, and their scent; and frankly, in a life that hasn't
very much spare time to do gardening, they do give so little trouble
once you remember to prune them at the right time, and to feed them
from time to time. Roses, too, surely bring back so many different
thoughts of so many different people. When Sir James Barrie gave
that great speech on *Courage*, to the students of St. Andrews he said,
"God gave us memory so that we might have roses in December."
And then he added, "In my experience – and you will find in the end
that it is yours also – the people I have cared for most and who have
seemed most worth caring for – my December roses – have been very
simple folk."

These roses in December, what wonderful things they are if you
come to think of them. What a wonderful storehouse of memories are
filed away in so mysterious a way in each of us. When friends get
together there's the inevitable "Do you remember?"; and when
friends depart there is the inevitable, "I remember." And we all have
our memories stored away. Not least do I remember the times when
we were all up against it and every day seemed quite possibly to be
our last day, and when we thought, "Well, if I get through this I'll try
to be different."

That broken home, that lost friendship, that empty chair! Roses in
December. There's a lovely story which I heard from Alastair
MacLean about Edmund Morell, who though a very left-wing politi-
cal leader was a great friend of the then Conservative Prime Minister,
Stanley Baldwin. On one occasion Morell was staying with Lord

Baldwin at Chequers and he told him all the things he had seen that made him so discontented and so upset, and so worried about life, so disgruntled; and Baldwin turned to Morell and picked up a bowl of roses and said, "Do you like roses, Morell?" and Morell said, "Like them! I love them." "Then," said Baldwin, "bury your face in this loveliness and thank God." There's something very wonderful in that story. Somewhere, as MacLean put it, there is "a harbour where the voice of the tempest is stilled." Stormy waters are not stormy every-where.

So may I leave you with this thought for today: if ever you are feeling down and disheartened, and perhaps even in despair about something or somebody, will you think of all the lovely memories that remain – your roses in December – and go out this day with greater courage and cheerfulness and hope – and thank God.

And God bless you and all those whom you love, wherever they may be.

What Helps to Keep us Going

Just after the Second World War finished and I got back from it all I was offered a disused farmhouse set lonely in the Lammermuir Hills and I fitted it up with fifty old air raid shelter beds; and for two glorious years we had it as an additional Camp centre for our Club. I wanted to get to know the boys again for I had been away for so long and the fourteen-year-olds had been eight or nine when I last saw them.

We were later to enlarge the Camp site by the sea we had before the war and set it up with a Cross overlooking it, in memory of "those who had loved to camp there and gave their lives that others too might love it" – as so many have done since. And under that Cross which looks towards the East where the sun rises and the sea beats on the shore below, we have these words: "When the morning was come they saw Jesus standing on the shore."

Camp teaches the art of how to live together and how to get to know each other as few other ways can; and I soon began to know the

Club boys again — but not always at first to their amusement or their pleasure! For example, one day I found some of the quite young ones smoking cigarettes; and I don't think they liked me very much for a few minutes after that! And after they recovered I told them — in that superior way that we pipe-smokers have — that in any case people, if they are going to smoke at all, ought to smoke a pipe and keep off cigarettes, and, lighting my pipe, I left it at that.

A few days later I came upon them again; and, bless me if they weren't all smoking pipes! Slightly misunderstanding me, they had gone into the nearby town of Dunbar and bought cheap pipes and even cheaper tobacco. Well, I took their pipes and said I'd give them back to them to give to their fathers when they got home, and I took their tobacco and gave them some sweets in exchange — though having sampled the tobacco I rather wished I'd kept the sweets. "But *you*

smoke a pipe, sir," they said, and I explained when they were older they might do so too – but not yet. And yet, you know, these words "but you smoke a pipe" jolted me a bit. It didn't mean that I gave up smoking my pipe (which perhaps you think I ought to have done and perhaps you are right!) but it did bring home to me again how easily and often unconsciously younger people can follow older people, and how much more careful older people ought to be. How is it, for example, that some very young children use such filthy and obscene language (without having the slightest idea what it means) if they hadn't picked it up from older people, perhaps even from their own parents?

You may remember a lovely story in the old Testament when Ruth turns to her friend and says, "Thy people shall be my people and thy God my God." Now, what kind of a God, for example, are we passing on to those who love us and trust us and look to us for a lead and an example?

I don't suppose many people nowadays, not even divinity students, read The Confessions of St. Augustine. It's a pity, because there are some great passages in it. That wonderful bit, for example, about how his mother brought him gradually from his sinful ways (for few saints are born with haloes, you know – indeed it has been said that the saints are the sinners who went on trying). And she began to do this by first of all beginning with herself. He wouldn't lisen to her advice and so she kept on praying for him; you know there are places, homes, and people whom you can reach at times only through prayer. And Augustine, like, I'm afraid, so many young people in every age, still took almost a delight in boasting that he was no end of a fellow; but he knew, nevertheless, that she prayed and watched and loved. And at last he had to return that love – for love is just like that. And so it was that later her God became his God.

Now I don't care who you are, I'm sure there must be someone watching you like that, either praying for you or following your example, taking your God as his or her God. It may be a little child, your own child perhaps; even someone who has left home – they are praying for you still, you know. It may be perhaps someone whom you are not even thinking about at the moment. Perhaps that is what is helping us to keep going:

Yes, we are always wondering, wondering, "How?"
Because we do not see

Someone, unknown perhaps, and far away,
On bended knee.

And perhaps before the work of the new day starts we might just for a minute too "bend the knee" and ask God to bless and give peace to someone we love.

Never Lonely or Forsaken

Those of us who knew what it was like to serve together, remember with gratitude that wonderful spirit of comradeship of those days that could scarcely today be equalled. Everyone seemed to be trying their best and people discovered, perhaps for the first time, that some whom they had previously thought so different from themselves were at heart very much the same, whatever our different denominations were or our political parties or even our football teams. That, I think, is what they miss most and perhaps miss only, when old soldiers talk about the war years. We all got to know each other better in these days, probably more than at any other time, probably because we were all in it together with one common aim and one common purpose, and each was prepared to carry his own pack and, if need be, the other fellow's too, and the tired man helped the man more tired and the hungry man shared with the man more hungry. Certainly my own battalion was like that and when we eventually were ordered out to France in the days after Dunkirk – too late, as it turned out, to be of much use – we went out as a large and on the whole a very happy family. It was not long before we were ordered back and it was while on our way back that something happened which I want to tell you about.

It was a Sunday evening and because we were all so very much on the move and because we had to keep fairly scattered because of enemy action, it had not been possible to have a service. So the medical officer and I along with our drivers decided we would have a short service just outside a wood, at which we would represent the Battalion.

We were just going to start the service when a young dispatch rider came along beside us and asked if he could join in too. He said to me, "before you begin I wonder if you could please remember to pray especially for all the folk at home for I know they'll be so worried about us. It doesn't really matter so much about us, does it? It is them we should be thinking about most, isn't it?" So we prayed under the trees that summer evening in June 1940 for our comrades around us and we especially remembered all those whom we loved at home or wherever they were, who we knew would be wondering and worrying about what was happening to us.

Very shortly after the service the young dispatch rider was killed; and when we got back eventually to England I wrote and told his people how his last thoughts had been about them and not about himself, and how he had been worried in case they were worried about him, and how his mind had been put at rest and at ease, knowing that his prayers had gone out for them.

I often think about that young dispatch rider and about my devoted young driver who too has joined that "great company whom no man can number", and when I think of all the unselfishness we knew and contrast it with so much selfishness that is so prevalent all around us, so often thinking of ourselves and how things are going to affect *us* and not thinking perhaps nearly enough about others until perhaps it is too late.

Now, there are among my old photographs and souvenirs constant memories of those whom I shall see no longer on this earth. That, in a way, is one of the misfortunes of getting even a little older each year – rather like the hour hand of the clock which never *seems* to move yet which an hour from now will be sixty minutes ahead. Even you and I will soon be nearly five minutes older than we were when I began to talk to you. To lose from earthly sight friends and loved ones, then, is one of the signs that we are due one day – sooner or later, not one of us knows when – to follow them. So I make no apology for saying more about what we call death – because it at least has a common interest to us all, and not, as I hope to show you, a morbid interest, nor is something to make us sad. There was rather a lovely play on television which some of you may have seen about an old man dying, and saying to a young girl who loved him, "Don't go to the funeral, my dear, because I won't be there." And all of us know what he meant by that – even though most of us feel that when we can we should go to the funeral as a matter of respect and remembrance, even though he or she is "not there". Where, if *he* won't be there, will he be? The Christian Church has surely most wisely never given a detailed answer to that question: it has done something better, it has given us the assurance that they are "in the hands of God". That is all we need to know, all we have a right to know. Yet, though there is no more that needs to be added to that, the Church does give its faithful people some further assurances. We believe, for example, in what the Church calls "the resurrection of the body"; which sometimes those who don't try to understand the Church's teaching *think* means the resurrection of the *corpse*. Man is body and soul – both living.[1] What the Church means – shortly – is that *you* will still be recognisable as *you* – and what makes you immediately recognisable from someone else is your body.

The Church believes that the dead and the living are one family under God the Father. They are still interested in us as we in them. "Let us, then, learn that we can never be lonely or forsaken in this life. . . . Shall they," said Cardinal Manning once, "love us less because they now have power to love us more?" If we remembered them in our prayers while they were alive on earth why should we not remember them still – alive in God's nearer presence. "They are in the hands of God"; and so, too, I pray are my friends in Canada, New Zealand, or wherever they may be.

What we call death is just a part of growing up, a fearless venture into the unknown which all must face. Death is only a fearful thing to those who do not believe this or who are afraid to face a loving Father.

And so in this world we are to be obedient and faithful to the task God has given to each one of us, however great or humble or seemingly insignificant that task may be.

One of the most moving services I have ever attended was in Florence in the last few weeks of the war. It was a service of confirmation taken by the late Archbishop of York, Dr Garbett. A great number of sun-tanned, weather-beaten young men in the prime of life, wearing khaki drill shorts and open-necked shirts, straight from the battle line, and straight to return there, went forward and knelt, were

[1] The above is an obvious simplification: may I suggest you read in, say, J. B. Phillip's translation, I Corinthians 15: 35 onwards, where you will see that the earthly body and the heavenly are not in competition, but each has its own splendour.

confirmed in Christ's name and blessed. And the Archbishop took as
his text, "Be thou faithful unto death and I will give you a crown of
life" – "*Of life.*" And many that day asked for life and God gave it to
them – even length of days for ever and ever.

All sorrow at partings, however temporary, is real and right, and
only the hard and callous do not feel it. But these partings are but
temporary. And let us never forget that however much we love those
whom we call our own, they are but lent on earth to us by God who
loves them even more; they are in His hands where no torment can
touch them.

God bless you and all whom you love, wherever – yes wherever –
they may be.

When only our Feet are Tired

I don't know about you, but I feel that few of us *walk* enough nowadays. And yet there are few things healthier – or more enjoyable –
than a good walk. At our Club winter camp we always tried to go a
really good walk on the first day of the year whatever the weather;
we start off often rather cold and uncomfortable and frankly wondering why on earth we are going when we could so easily sit round a
nice warm log fire; but by the time we get back we're warm and
glowing and so glad we went. I remember once, after such a long
winter walk, asking one of the smaller boys how he felt, "Are you
feeling very tired?" I asked him, and I'll never forget his reply, "Only
my feet, sir." It's a great thought that at the end of a long day's
journey only our feet are tired; now isn't it?

If you come to think of it life is a journey, whether long or short,
we all have to make; and then one day we turn the bend on the road
and are lost to sight for a time. We call that journey along the road
life, and the bend on the way death. As I talk to you now, there are
two things only I know about you for certain – one is that you are
alive, or at least living – and I hope alive – and the other is that one
day you, like me, will turn that bend on the road we call death –

there is nothing more certain than death; in fact we often use the expression ourselves – "as sure as death".

Now a lot of people who lack faith (for faith is the opposite of fear) get frightened about this – especially for those whom they love. So I want to give you one of the best pieces of news that ever was given to the world: "Neither life nor death can ever separate us from the love of God." As friends in life are bound together across the world by the unseen chain of God's love, so too are friends in what we call death, for "neither life nor death can ever separate us".

Now, when you come to think of it, life would not only be hopeless but nonsense unless we believed that. I can't believe that a bit of metal shaped like a bullet, a street accident, a crash, a virus or whatever it may be can ever finish for good the real life of that person I knew and know still. Though for me now his friendly laughter be silenced, his boyish joy for the lovely things in the world around be but a memory; though for me now his love of music be only as a dream and his delight in simple things and his childlike faith, I know that they whom I know and love can never die.

> In the eyes of the foolish they seem to have died,
> And their journey was accounted to be their hurt,
> And their journeyings away from us to be their ruin;
> But they are in peace.

Nor can I believe that your life or mine can ever be fully finished here. There are so many things to do, and the days pass so quickly. And I don't believe that God ever meant anything in this world to be left unfinished – not even such small things as you and me. He is our Father and I just can't believe that what, for want of a better word, we call death, can ever bring His children to an end.

You may remember how the young student, Malcolm, in one of George MacDonald's books said to his teacher, "But, sir, isn't death a dreadful thing?" And the master replied, "That depends on whether a man regards it as his fate or as the will of a perfect God . . . if God be Light then Death itself must be full of splendour. . . ."

So we should have no fear of death either for ourselves or for those whom we love. That doesn't mean that it's wrong to be sorry when someone we love turns the bend of the road and is lost for a time to one's sight. He has gone on a journey which one day we all must take; and even the bravest folk then cannot hold back a tear or feel a lump rising in the throat:

We who are left, how shall we look again
Happily on the sun or feel the rain
Without remembering how they who went
Ungrudgingly and spent
Their lives for us, loved too the sun and rain?

A bird among the rain-wet lilac sings
But we, how shall we turn to little things
And listen to the birds and winds and streams
Made holy by their dreams
Nor feel the heartbreak in the heart of things?[2]

But it does mean that we should have no fear – and that's quite a different thing.

And for ourselves, let us pray God that at the end of the day only our feet are tired.

Some Kinship with the Divine

He was one of the most difficult boys I have ever had. Not only could he do little that was right; he did quite a bit that was wrong, and one of his specialities was in thieving. Mind you he had a strange honour to himself in his thieving for he nearly always gave away what he had taken. He came, as so many did in these days, from a very poor home; there was no money or employment and the whole family lived in one room. Though he had no money he quite clearly wanted to be generous, and anything he took as he explained to me once, was always, as he put it, "from those who could afford it". Nor did he confine his stealing to taking things from *people*.

Once at a Camp he brought me two duck eggs for my breakfast and I asked him where he had got them from and he said, not surprisingly, "from a duck". So even the ducks did not get off with it when he was around. I told him to put the eggs back at once and delivered

[2] Wilfred Wilson Gibson.

my usual short sermon on the evil of stealing things – all of which he had heard before and I could not help feeling was to him – well, rather like water off a duck's back! Well he went away and in about five minutes he came back and said to me that he didn't know which duck he had taken them from because they all looked so much alike, and in any case they all looked perfectly happy and he thought I may as well take the eggs and be done with it.

Well that was the kind of chap he was and I will never forget how he impressed – not entirely favourably – the local Laird, who for fairly obvious reasons, had got to know him quite well by this time, since, among other things, he had without invitation picked a considerable number of gooseberries; and yet he liked the boy because one could not help liking him.

I wouldn't have called him in any sense "religious"; he didn't seem to take much interest when, for example, we had prayers each night in the Club Chapel or at Camp, and one could not help feeling perhaps that some of his prayers were not quite the same as ours. But there, as in so many other cases and at so many other times before and since, I found I was wrong, and some of you may remember how I found this.

I knew when war came he had joined up somewhere, and I knew too that he was in the Far East. Apart from that I knew nothing about him; and of course I didn't expect to hear from him; he wasn't the kind of chap who wrote letters. Then one day I did hear from him and it surprised me a lot and pleased me even more; but he told me that this would probably be the last time I would hear from him, that they were being surrounded, that there was no possible chance of getting away, that he hoped to get this out with a runner who was going back to Headquarters, and that he hoped I would receive it because he wanted to say "thank-you" for all that the friendship of the Club had meant to him and to say that he was sorry if he had been a bit of a nuisance at times. And then he added in his rather sprawly writing, "If there is one thing that comforts and has been able to carry me through more than anything else it is that prayer we used to say so often in the Club Chapel – 'Teach us, Almighty Father, to serve Thee more faithfully, to give and not to count the cost, to fight and not to heed the wounds, to toil and not to seek for rest, to labour and not to ask for any reward – save that of knowing that we do Thy will.'"

So I remember him and how I had thought all these years had

been wasted, and how wrong I had been. "There is in all men," remember how John Buchan wrote once, "even the basest, some kinship with the Divine . . . the task of leadership is not to put greatness into humanity but to elicit it, for the greatness is there already." So may I leave you now with some words of the beloved Arthur Stanton:

> When the Lord Jesus Christ wanted to make some poor fishermen apostles, martyrs, saints, although they were a miserable set of men – you know what they did, they all ran away when He was in trouble – they never understood Him – they left Him, were very backward to believe in Him – He wanted to make those men apostles, martyrs and saints, and He said to them, "Ye are the light of the world," and they became the light of the world.

You never can tell, you see, you never can tell.

The Givers and the Getters

You may remember how it was said that the boys of Rugby used to say in the days of their great Headmaster, Dr Arnold (whom you can read about in *Tom Brown's Schooldays*), "You can never tell old Arnold a lie, because he always believes a fellow." If someone knows that you really trust him he is not likely to let you down. (Of course there are some exceptions to this as there are to everything else, but I think you will agree that it is nearly always worth while risking the exceptions.)

I have always trusted boys with money, for example; and I don't like to *think* that they have ever let me down. I never count change, for example, and they get to know this; and yet, of course, there are exceptions here too, and I would like to tell you now of a notable exception.

Again I am back in my old Battalion. For a short time we ran a sort of cycling club and during times off some of us used to explore the Norfolk countryside, where we were for a time stationed. I remember the Colonel coming to see us off on our first excursion – Freddie

Johnston was just that kind of a Colonel, always interested in what we were doing, always encouraging.

Well, on this particular day we cycled a good way and were feeling pretty exhausted. So we stopped at a canteen and I gave my young Corporal, who was one of my old Club boys, a pound note and told him to go and get some tea and buns for us all. We got the tea and buns and the Corporal, a really fine fellow who was later killed in action, handed me back my change – all in silver. Now, for some reason or other I thought that the change looked rather a lot and also out of a certain amount of curiosity as to what the canteen had in fact

charged for the tea and buns, I unusually counted the change – and it came to exactly £1! I looked at the Corporal: "Well you see," he said, "we didn't want you to spend your money on us, but we wanted you to think that you had." Yes, I was glad I counted the change that day; for you see they hoped that I would not know that they had paid for their own tea and buns, and not only that, but for mine too. And that is what I mean when I talk about the spirit of true comradeship – the spirit that makes it a joy to give without expecting or wanting thanks, but just for the sake of making someone happy.

There is a somewhat similar incident told by Lord Ballantrae in his book, *The Trumpet in the Hall*, when the wind blew away all the money he was carrying for his Company's pay – mostly in ten shilling notes – and in a very short time every note was returned to him, though so much could so easily have gone astray without anyone knowing who had taken it.

It reminds me too of the story I was told once about George Hirst, the famous Yorkshire and English cricketer. When he retired he became a cricket coach at Eton where he was very much loved and respected, and the time came for him to retire from that too, and he was playing his last match. And suddenly the boys of Eton who were playing that day thought it would be rather a lovely thing if George Hirst could finish his career by taking a hat-trick, and so they arranged that he would take his hat-trick – and he did. And George Hirst went off the field smiling, pretending that he did not know that it had all been arranged to make him happy. Because, of course, he was far too good a cricketer to be taken in.

Sir Alexander Paterson, the great prison reformer, once said, "You may divide Gaul into three parts, and the compass into four; you may cut all the earth into five continents; but there are only two sorts of men – the givers and the getters."

And so I wonder if we could ask ourselves quite simply today: what kind of person am I? Do I trust or distrust people? or better perhaps – can I myself be trusted? Am I a giver (not caring who gets the credit) or am I a getter? I am sure the answer to these questions, if honestly answered, will depend a lot on whether we are happy people or not.

Seven Scots

All these were broadcast either on radio or TV. The talk on Earl Haig is based on the talk given at the Anniversary Service at Dryburgh Abbey, that on Sir Walter Scott was given at the Edinburgh Academy on its 150th Anniversary Service in a fuller form, the talk on Robert Louis Stevenson was first given in a longer form to the Edinburgh R.L.S. Club, and the talk on Jimmie Dalgleish was broadcast the week after he was killed beside me during the war. The talk on Robert Burns was first given to the Coldstream Burns Club and has been used several times since in a longer form.

Robert Burns
(1759–1796)

I've sat by a Lowland burn talking about Burns – or listening rather –
as a young soldier talked and quoted poem after poem until the mid-
summer night turned violet-pink and the piper played "Lochaber no
more" and it was time to lie down and sleep on the heather of the
Lammermoors – our bed for the night; and I've heard men in Cairo,
in Hong Kong, and by the banks of the Arno near Florence talk of
their "brither Scot" as though in fact he were their brother; and I've
heard his songs sung by boys from poor and sunless streets of our big
towns, at camp now, their white faces turning brown; and I've heard
them sung by stiff dressed choirs and moving the hearts of even stiffer
audiences. I've listened to him being quoted by an old gardener who
claimed to know all his works, and listened to a rich and influential
Laird read – after dinner that had followed a day on the hills with the
gun – Tam Samson's Elegy, with the tears running down his cheeks
(though his wife said it was the port, he and I knew it was the genius
of Burns):

> Ilk hoary hunter mourned a brither;
> Ilk sportsman youth bemoaned a father;
> Yon auld gray stane, among the heather,
> Marks out his head.

Of course there are still quite a number of people who, while
having to admit that Burns wrote some lovely things, feel some aren't
altogether quite "proper" as he himself wasn't quite "proper".

But remember how the late Lord Rosebery pointed out, in that
often quoted and, I hope, often read speech given on the hundredth
anniversary of the poet's death, that he should like to go a step further
and affirm that we should have something to be grateful for even in
the weakness of men like Burns . . . "How shall we judge a giant great

in gifts and great in temptation; great in strength and great in weakness? Let us glory in his strength and be comforted in his weakness. And when we thank heaven for the inestimable gift of Burns, we do not need to remember wherein he was imperfect, we cannot bring ourselves to regret that he was made of the same clay as ourselves."

I've heard Robert Burns being described as an untypical Scot – for Burns was no Puritan; but rather would I describe Burns as a *real* Scot, *because* he was no Puritan. G. K. Chesterton was right when he said that Puritanism was a disguise that did not fit the Scottish temperament. Puritanism was an English export to Scotland, and Cromwell drove this export in a way that would gladden the heart of any Chancellor of the Exchequer. Puritanism is not native to Scotland. Its very definition in the Oxford Dictionary links it with English Protestantism. The very worship and architecture of still so many Scottish Kirks is but an English Puritan hangover and about as far removed from the Church of the Reformation as from the Church of Rome. And yet, just because Puritanism is but skin deep in the Scottish character while we stand when in court the representative of the law enters, we still find congregations sitting while the representative of the Gospel enters – lest by any chance such outward action in the Kirk might be regarded as ritual and rather "popish"; yet what Scotsman doesn't stand whenever the haggis enters? We banish prayers to the saints, but with almost religious fervour we address the same haggis. Prayers for the dead are looked upon as suspect and smell faintly of Rome; but when Burns addresses Mary in Heaven, no word is raised in protest and something in the heart of every man rises with the beauty, in communion with the beauty, of it.

> Thou ling'ring star, with less'ning ray
> That lovst to greet the early morn,
> Again thou usher'st in the day
> My Mary from my soul was torn.
> O Mary! dear departed shade!

A prayer to the dead; but in poetry and by Burns and so it's all right!

A strange race we Scots, where the cold bleakness of the Kirk so often bans all ritual and "colour", yet the colourful ritual of Freemasonry thrives behind closed doors as nowhere else in the world!

Then that kist o' whistles[1] formerly purged with puritan pride, once given even the tiniest loophole now forms the central object of adoration in so many sanctuaries. Truly in Sir William Gilbert's words: "Our air severe is but a mere veneer." Burns knew the real Scot as few have done before or since his time; and Burns hated veneers and any form of hypocrisy. No real Scottish hero was a Puritan however varied these heroes have been – Knox, or Montrose, Bonnie Prince Charlie, Robert Louis Stevenson or J. M. Barrie, or the pride of our Borders, Sir Walter Scott. To quote Chesterton again: "No Scottish Puritan could possibly have been the Scottish Poet." We in Scotland still suffer from a hangover – and our hangover is Cromwellian! It is we who are untypical Scots, not Burns:

> O Scotia, my dear my native soil!
> For whom my warmest wish to heaven is sent!
> Long may thy hardy sons of rustic toil
> Be blest with health and peace, and sweet content!

There are, it seems to me, three great beacons of light that Robert Burns has given us and – for such is genius – they still shine as beacons today.

And first, for it is the most important of all, to the home. A nation that loses its sense of the primacy of the home loses its soul. And too often today what was once "ma hame" has become "ma hoose". Burns knew the meaning of home:

> To make a happy fireside clime
> To weans and wife,
> That's the true pathos and sublime
> of human life.

Or the perhaps better known and almost perfect description of family life as it ought to be, as depicted by Burns in the Cottar's Saturday Night:

> Th' expectant wee things, toddlan', stacher through
> To meet their Dad, wi' flickerin' noise and glee.
> His wee-bit ingle, blinkin' bonnilie,
> His clean hearth-stane, his thrifty wifie's smile,
> The lispin' infant, prattlin' on his knee.

Burns has given us a picture of home life which Scotland would do well to copy again; and even when the father in Burns did stray from the straight and narrow path – like Tam o' Shanter – he was at

[1] Organ.

least returning to his *own* wife even though she's a –

   . . . sulky sullen dame,
   Gathering her brows like gathering storm,
   Nursing her wrath to keep it warm.

And to Burns a real home meant religion in the home. His letter to Alexander Cunningham – which should be read by all who would dare to say that Burns was not a religious man – contains this sentence, "I will deeply imbue every child of mine with religion." He wrote that four years before he died. Does it ever strike you why for so long the doors of the Scottish Kirk – which should now all be open – were closed on week days was because, while on Sunday the whole community came as a family to God's House, on the other days of the week each fireside became an altar, each father a priest? Burns calls us back to a true sense of religion which abolished cant and humbug and gives us an honest clean Gospel (and not the least honest bit about it being that however hard we try, we are but poor examples of it).

John Buchan in his fine life of Sir Walter Scott, tells how the Church in Burns' day was deeply estranged to that which was vital in the national life. It was that estrangement that he attacked with all its attendant cant and hypocrisies. Burns recalled us to a true conception of religion – not just a Sunday parade. Burns tells us to show forth our faith in its true colours:

   All hail religion! Maid divine!
   Pardon a muse sae mean as mine,
   Who in her rough imperfect line
   Thus daurs to name Thee;
   To stigmatise *false friends* of thine
   Can ne'er defame thee.

And lastly, Burns calls us back to a true sense of loyalty to our land and to the true meaning of that oft-abused word, democracy. That we should:

   Preserve the dignity of man
   With soul erect.

He hated class war and that modern version of it – inverted snobbery. He was an individualist in the very best sense of the word; he took a man for what he was worth, be he rich or poor.

He loved true liberty, he hated anarchy (that oft disguised name for liberty in certain quarters today).

Be anarchy cursed, and be tyranny damned;
And who would to Liberty e'er be disloyal
May his son be a hangman – and he his first trial.

How he would have hated the concentration camps, the suppression of free speech, the growth of covetousness, the perversion of truth; these monsters which are rearing their ugly heads today. A member of the Home Guard of his day, he was loyal to true democracy (somewhat new in its conception in his day) and to an ordered and constitutional Government.

The wretch that would a tyrant own,
And the wretch, his true born brother,
Who would set the mob aboon the throne,
May they be damned together.

A true patriot who loved his country – he was not a narrow nationalist or, which comes to the same thing, a provincial racialist.

O let us not, like snarling tykes,
In wrangling be divided;
'Till slap! – come in an unco loon,
And wi' a rung decide it:
Be Britain still to Britain true,
Amang oursel's united;
For never but by British hands
Maun British wrangs be righted.

And lastly may I remind you all again – if reminding it is – of the story of one of the Belles of Mauchline? You may recall his rhyme about them:

Miss Miller is fine, Miss Markland's divine,
Miss Smith she has wit, and Miss Betty is braw;
There's beauty and fortune to get wi' Miss Morton,
But Armour's the jewel for me o' them a'.

A. A. Thomson tells us how the six Mauchline belles lived their lives in sunshine or rain, riches or poverty, joy or sorrow. One became immortal. To all of them the greatest thing in their lives was that they had known one man. Some of them lived to a great age. Seventy years after the jingle had been written, the old woman who had been the beautiful Miss Morton lay dying. Her grandchildren stood round the bed. Waiting for the end, they spoke in hushed voices of old times.

"Do you", asked one of them, "remember Robert Burns?"

A smile lit the drawn and wrinkled face, dying lips moved: "Aye", she said, "brawly that!"

Do we again today remember the light that shines from Robert Burns — one who had the heart of a man in him?

Aye, brawly that . . .

Sir Walter Scott
(1771–1832)

As you probably know, had not Sir Walter Scott at the age of 18 months developed a lame leg, he might have become a soldier and not that lad of Abbotsford who gave Scotland such a reputation for good, for in many quarters Scotland is known quite simply as "the land of Scott". Yet he always remained a soldier at heart and showed more than the ordinary courage of a soldier. How great were his campaigns and how gallantly he fought them: "I am very ill today", he wrote once, "with rheumatic headache and a still more vile affection which fills my head with pain, my heart with sadness, and my eyes with tears; I worked, therefore, all this forenoon." Though he was essentially a very fit man, strong and robust (it called for a strong man to do all the work he did, rising every morning at 6 a.m., writing hard, attending the Courts and all the rest of it) there were times when he suffered badly from a violent cramp. For example, he wrote The Bride of Lammermoor sometimes in such suffering that he could not always next day remember what he had written, and had to read it through to see where he left off in case he had written nonsense.

Then, surely everyone knows about his great losses that "turned his necessity to glorious gain"; how he had put his money into the firm of his old schoolfriend of Kelso days, James Ballantyne, the printer, and giving most of the capital needed to set up John Ballantyne, James's brother, as a publisher; and how, in the course of quite a few years the publishing firm was so in debt that failure stared him in the face. How, again, with hard work, he overcame this difficulty until a great financial crisis came in 1825 when he learned that Constable, his chief publisher, along with James Ballantyne, now his partner, would be bankrupt. You find him writing this: "Ballantyne called on me this morning; my extremity has come, I suppose it has involved my all." And then he pictured the scene if he had got to give up his beloved Abbotsford. Typically he remembers his dogs, how they would sit in vain for him. He mentions them first: "poor things, I must get them fine masters". Then he remembers his beloved servants, Will Laidlaw and Tom Purdie. It is true to the character of the man that he never seemed to bear John Ballantyne any grudge, but loved him to the end. And, as he stood by his grave beside my old Church in the Canongate, and the cloudy sky suddenly cleared, remembering the cheerfulness and affection of his departed friend and forgetting all else, with tears in his eyes he whispered to his son-in-law, "I feel as if there would be less sunshine for me from this day forth."

The most striking thing of all, I always feel, is the way his servants remained loyal even when they must have known that he could no longer pay them; and characteristically one of his greatest comforts was the love of his dogs. Typically they appeared in some of his portraits; one is with him at his feet at his statue in the Scott Monument in Edinburgh. There was Camp, for instance. He always talked to Camp as if he understood what was said. And the servant as he was laying the cloth for dinner would say, "Camp, my good fellow, the Sheriff's coming home by the ford (or by the hill)", and the sick animal would bestir himself to welcome his master, going out of the back or the front door according to the direction given. When Camp died, he was buried on a beautiful moonlight night in the little garden behind the house, opposite the window at which Scott usually sat writing. Sir Walter Scott's daughter told her husband, who wrote his Life, that she remembers how the whole family stood in tears around Camp's grave as her father smoothed down the turf, looking sadder than she had ever seen him look. He had an important dinner engagement that day and had asked to be excused, apologising because of the "death of a dear old friend".

He spent his last days at Abbotsford, having been rushed back ill and dying from a tour on the Continent, Abbotsford — the place which of all places he loved best. There, with the delight at being home, he recovered slightly, glad to see the friends he loved so much, and glad to be back again in his beloved Border country. He tried to write but his now feeble fingers failed. He was taken through the gardens in a chair; he sat in the library at the centre window that he might see the Tweed flowing past. And when he asked Lockhart to read to him, and Lockhart asked him which book he should read, Scott replied, "Need you ask? There is but one." And so, from all the great library at Abbotsford he chose the one book and read to him from St. John's Gospel. And, as he lay dying, his last words were spoken to Lockhart: "I may have but a minute to speak to you. Be a good man; be virtuous; be religious; be a good man; nothing else will give you any comfort when you come to lie here." So, in the afternoon on the 21st September 1832, this good man died in the home he loved and with those he loved around him. It was a beautiful warm day – so warm that every window was wide open – and so still that the Tweed could be heard rippling gently over the pebbles.

David Livingstone
(1813–1873)

Surely David Livingstone was one of the greatest Scotsmen who has ever lived.

Just think for a moment of his terrific courage, his dogged perseverance, his burning indignation against wrong, his toughness, his gentleness, his hatred of cant and humbug and sickly sentimentality, his love of beautiful things, his despising of cheap popularity, his utter disregard of wealth or false security or easy comfortableness – these and many more qualities are but the ingredients of this true Christian warrior who was at the same time the true Christian gentleman.

He loved life in all its glory, in all its simplicity, with all its fun, with all its sadness, with all its companionship, with all its loneliness, with all its challenge . . . yes, with all its challenge. Surely here too was a man who dwelt in a tent but sought a city whose maker and builder is God; and, as he put it himself, "I am willing to go anywhere – provided it be forward." As Dr Kirk, one of his companions in the early journeys of exploration was to write later, "D.L. is a most unsafe leader. He never thinks of getting back."

There are so many stories about him but may I just give you what is probably the best-known incident in all his life. There was a time when things looked extremely difficult and dangerous – even more difficult and dangerous than some of his usual experiences, and that was saying something. This time the chief he met looked as though he were going to be extremely difficult. Livingstone had a river to cross and he needed canoes to cross it and the chief gathered his warriors from all sides. No women were to be seen which meant that their purpose was quite clearly to divide Livingstone's party and to set on them when they crossed the next day. They say that this was the only time that Livingstone was afraid, for normally he never bothered about danger. He thought perhaps he might cross during the night, and sitting in his tent wrote this in his diary: "Evening. Felt much turmoil of spirit in view of having all my plans for the welfare of this region and teeming population knocked on the head by savages tomorrow. But I read that Jesus came and said 'all power is given unto him in heaven and earth, go ye therefore and teach all nations and [heavily underlined] lo, I am with you always even unto the end of the world'. It's a word of a gentleman of the most sacred and strictest honour and there is an end on it. I will not cross furtively by night as intended. It would appear as flight and why should such a man as I flee? . . . I shall take observation for latitude and longitude tonight though they may be my last: I am quite calm now. Thank God." So he closed his diary for the night and went to sleep. But in the morning things looked worse than ever; the number of the warriors had swollen and only one canoe had been given them, no others could be seen. The situation was quite critical, yet quietly and calmly they strike camp and pack their baggage as though nothing were the matter. One canoe is sent backwards and forwards from the side of the river while Livingstone stands beside the warriors on the bank. He keeps them amused and shows them his watch, and his mirror, his burning-glass, and then when the last man has got into the canoe he thanks the chief for his great kindness in lending it to him and steps aboard, confident, you see, all the time in that word of a gentleman.

And then there is the lovely story told by Bishop Maples of his meeting some years after Livingstone's death in the heart of Africa with an old native who, bowing to him, presented him with an old worn coat given, he said, ten years before (the coat can now be seen at the Livingstone Memorial at Blantyre) by "a white man who treated black men as brothers and whose memory would be cherished along the Rovuma River after we were all dead. A short man with a bushy moustache and keen piercing eye, whose words were always gentle and whose manners were always kind, whom as a leader it was a privilege to follow, and who knew the way to the heart of all men."

Remember that we too can go forth in the strength of Him who carried Livingstone in all his ways however hard – the strength of his Master whom he so faithfully followed, his Master and ours, his Lord and ours "who treats all men as brothers whose memory will be cherished after we are all dead . . . whom it is a privilege to follow and who knows the way to the heart of all men". For the secret of all true and great leadership is to see through the leader Him whom he follows:

So from your life He beckons me
And from your heart His love is shed
Till I lose sight of you and see
The Christ instead.

Such is David Livingstone – and such surely is leadership.

Robert Louis Stevenson
(1850–1891)

Here is another great Scotsman who lived a very long time after St. Patrick but who also for different reasons had to leave Scotland. Robert Louis Stevenson, who was born in Edinburgh so recently that I have met people who knew him, and like so many Scottish boys, I suppose, I had read to me and learnt from early times the *Child's Garden of Verses* with its:

> Leary, leary, licht the lamp

and

> I have a little shadow
> that goes in and out with me

and

> The friendly cow all red and white
> I love with all my heart,
> She gives me cream with all her might
> To eat with apple tart.

or "The Swing Song" which my father once set to music, or:

> The world is so full of a number of things,
> I am sure we should all be as happy as kings.

and all the rest of it.

Now, here is the real genius of Stevenson that he really was a very sick man and yet he was able to write as he did. "Sick or well", he cried once — and very sick he was at the time — "sick or well, I have had a splendid life"; that's the real language of happiness. And, as Alistair Maclean once put it, "a religion that makes you genuinely happy is the only religion worth having". It was that feeling that the world was a happy place to live in and that people were nice people, and friendly people that gave one boy at least a brighter vision of life and a more ideal picture of people than he might otherwise have had and set him off at least with prejudice and faith in the inner goodness of man and the world around us, and not with a feeling that the world was a dismal dreary place. I think if you have that feeling you will always find that, though there are many bad and rotten things in the world, one never meets a really out and out bad man, not even in the worst of men; some good quality survives. That though, as the theologians tell us, there is original sin, there is too — what the theologians, alas, seldom tell us — original goodness in mankind. And Stevenson gives us that feeling; and adds to that however ill you or the world may be, there is always a place for a cheery smile and a heart full of courage. He showed it most in his life and he showed it too in his writings.

For we must remember that there is so much in Stevenson's life that could have made him sour and unhappy. So many of the things he loved he could not do, so many of the places he loved he had to leave.

How sad a picture really it is to see him waving goodbye to his beloved Edinburgh before he set out to the South Seas, or his memories
there of the places he loved as a boy.

Blows the wind today, and the sun and the rain are flying,
Blows the wind on the moors today and now,
Where above the graves of the martyrs, the whaups are crying,
My heart remembers how.

But even out in the South Seas in Samoa where he built his new
and final home, he found new life, new happiness, and above all, new
friends, though he never forgot his old ones. Tusitala, remember, they
called him – the Teller of Tales. And indeed he really did make it a
family and among the loveliest things he wrote and left are the prayers
he wrote for his "family". For that brave and happy life is summed up
morning and evening by his family prayers and perhaps most of all in
these precious words he wrote: "Grant us, O Lord, the gift of courage
and gaiety and a quiet mind."

His was a simple philosophy that is well within the reach of every
man. In our nursery at home we had on the fireplace an extract from
his Christmas sermon which soon I knew by heart. How I wish I could
live it as a man, as well as I learnt it as a small boy.

"To be honest, to be kind – to earn a little and to spend a little
less, to make upon the whole a family happier for his presence, to
renounce when that shall be necessary and not to be embittered, to
keep a few friends, but these without capitulation – above all, on the
same grim condition, to keep friends with himself – here is a task for
all that a man has of fortitude and delicacy."

His own epitaph too is simple and again within the reach surely of
most of us. "Here lies one who meant well, tried a little, failed much"
– and then he added, "surely that may be his epitaph of which he need
not be ashamed."

If R.L.S. "failed much" how much greater have we – most of us –
failed. Yet we have always this challenge and this consolation that,
as he put it, "to travel hopefully is a better thing than to arrive, and
true success is to labour".

We too can begin from now surely, to "travel hopefully" as he
did and so become more cheerful when we don't feel like being cheerful, and more happy when we are feeling rather miserable, and more
kind when we are too often indifferent, and more human when sometimes we are feeling rather cold. In other words, we can begin to find

our true success in labouring for the things for which he laboured and above all pray for the same gifts for which he prayed that they might be granted to us, as at the end of his days surely they were granted to him – the gifts of "courage and gaiety and the quiet mind".

Hely Hutchinson Almond
(1832–1903)

The match of the year is nearly over – and what a match it has been! Still the result is in doubt; and now there are only two minutes to go. Yet, the side with four points lead looks as though the game is theirs and that, taken all in all would, we think, be a pretty fair result. And then, just in the last minute one of those things happens; the losing side scores. The lead is now down to one point. All now depends on whether or not the try will be converted. Whatever happens now, one side is certain to lose by one point.

Over the cheering field there now falls a deadly hush; and then the ball goes between the posts and the whistle goes for time. The team that just two minutes before had been leading by four points, had now lost by one! Their Headmaster wonders what he will say, for as I have said, it is *the* match of the season – and just at the last minute too! And here is the Captain coming over to him. How, he wonders, will he put it to the Captain? Will it not be better just to begin by saying something like "bad luck" or would he . . . But there is no need to think what he is going to say, for the Captain is already saying to him: "Wasn't that a really grand game, sir? The best I have ever played in. Gosh, I wouldn't have missed it for anything." The Headmaster smiles as he turns away; they had lost . . . and in the last minute . . . and it was the best game he had ever played in, the Captain had said. He was glad the the Captain had spoken first.

That's what people still call "the school spirit"; it is a thing you really can't define. How does it come and where, for example, did the Captain of that particular school get it? I can't tell you; and the Headmaster, I am sure, can't tell you; and the boy couldn't tell you –

because he wouldn't know what you were talking about. But I am certain that in this case much of it goes back to the influence of a man who had died nearly fifty years before. For one of the surest tests of leadership lies in this – that when the time comes, as it comes to all, for the leader to rest from his labours, "his works do follow him".

This man's name was Hely Hutchinson Almond; and, though the school he moulded has purposely never been a very large school, it has done a tremendous amount to give to schools today that spirit which we always associate with the finest type of sportsmanship. Dr Almond is a very difficult kind of man to describe. Indeed, it seems almost an impertinence for anyone who does not come from his school to dare to try to describe him.

I heard once a story about a man who was crossing over the Dean Bridge in Edinburgh when a boy from Dr Almond's – or, as they used to call him, the Head's – school asked him if he could direct him to Raeburn Place. And the man said that he himself was going that way. And then he noticed that he had been to the same school, so he asked him if the Head had been doing anything odd recently. The boy showed surprise and indignation. What did this man mean by speaking to him so disrespectfully of the Head? "Well," said the man, "things must have changed because when I was at . . ." "Oh, I did not know that it is your school too, sir," said the boy. "In that case let me tell you what he did the other day . . ." For that was one of the surest ways of showing their loyalty or, if you like, their love for the Head. They would laugh among themselves at some of the extraordinary things he did – and he did some rather extraordinary things – among themselves, but not with those outside.

Now, what were some of the extraordinary things he did? Well, to us now, and largely because of him, they don't seem very extraordinary at all – in fact many of them seem only natural. They are the kind of things a boy just ought to do – open necks, plenty of exercise and fresh air, trust and responsibility for older boys and the frendliness which carries with it a respect that must always accompany real friendship – good manners, if you like, good manners which not only show a respect for others but self-respect. And with this a deep and abiding feeling of purpose in life, a purpose which isn't a selfish purpose but is out to give the best to the community in which you live, and which therefore begins by making yourself the best possible self you could be so as you would be a help and not a hindrance to the community. An emphasis on character, initiative and healthy living, and, as the successor of Almond once put it, "the problem of how to get a true view of ourselves". When Almond chose head boys, prefects, or whatever you would like to call them, he chose them for what he called the object for which such offices exist — "the order, tone, and morality of a school".

Many of these things, as I have said, we take for granted today; but they were certainly not taken for granted when Almond — fighting all the while an uphill battle against so many of the conventions of his age — began his great work. Many of these things we can no longer take for granted today because, with the stress that is laid now on putting before all else the passing of exams, it is not everywhere true that what counts is character or initiative or even clean living. Almond fought a battle, and sometimes a lone battle, and the school he founded still stands to "hold fast to that which is good". Too often now our schools, instead of being what Almond would call "nurseries of character", have become in this competitive, "rat race" age factories for just turning out passers — or failers! — in exams.

How, how did Almond do it all? First and foremost, I suppose he did it by personal example. He was what he was, not so much because he thought it, or wrote it, or spoke it, or theorised it, or argued it out — but just because he *was* it. And then he did it because he really cared for the good of each boy. Even when his hair and his beard had turned white on his manly head, he still had the heart of a boy; and when he said that he expected this and that from a boy he knew, too (and they knew, too), that he had always given this and that himself. He showed us that the way to get the best out of people is to expect the best from them, while always trying ourselves to be what we expect them to be.

Perhaps one of the best tributes paid to Almond is paid by one who belonged to the school's most deadly yet friendly rival — for that is praise indeed. Sir Robert Bruce Lockhart whose nephew became Head Master of Loretto later, remembering his days at Fettes recalls most vividly a visit from Almond. He mentions that it was in the Fettes Chapel that he heard the most inspiring preacher he had ever listened to, and this inspiring preacher was "the famous Dr Almond, the founder and the first Headmaster of Loretto". He had heard of him often from his father who had admired him greatly; and he had always thought of him as the man who had refereed the first "rugger" international between Scotland and England and who had caught what then ranked as the largest trout ever taken on a fly. He had always pictured him as a muscular Christian.

"He was an old man when I heard him preach at Fettes," Sir Robert wrote, "and his white beard gave him the appearance of an Old Testament patriarch. But there was a magnetism in his voice and in his eyes which held me spellbound. It had the same effect on the other boys and, during his sermon not a cough or a shuffle of feet was heard. His words made a lasting impression on me and almost made me wish that I hade gone to Loretto. The services in chapel are among my happiest memories of Fettes, and in those memories the dim incandescent lights shining on the venerable figure of the Loretto headmaster stand out as the symbol of the unfilled aspirations of my youth."

One can't help feeling that great as that influence was on that occasion, how much greater and more real must have been the influence of day-to-day contact during these most formulative years of a schoolboy.

How great is the responsibility of us all when it comes to the example we set, and the lead we give, to those younger than ourselves, whether as parents or older brothers and sisters or as friends or as teachers. No wonder a friend of St. Vincent de Paul once said: "To see money spent on teaching them merely to read and write without making them better Christians is a real pity and yet generally this is what happens. . . . I believe that if St. Paul and St. Denis were to come to France now, they would undertake the work of schoolmasters in preference to any other. . . . The School is the Noviciate of Christianity. It is the seminary of seminaries."

I am sure that Almond would have agreed with this. I am sure that it is from that that still can be found his influence, an influence so difficult to define or explain, but perhaps best summed up in some words of one of my Club boys who after the annual cricket visit to the school that Almond made, said to me: "Whenever I come back from Loretto somehow I always feel better." I can't help feeling that to hear that would have pleased Almond more than anything else.

Douglas Haig
(1861–1928)
Field-Marshal Earl Haig of Bemersyde, K.T., O.M.

In the heart of the Scottish Borders, among the green and friendly
hills, two great Borderers of evergreen memory lie buried side by side.
Walter Scott, the Laird of Abbotsford, and Douglas Haig, the Laird of
Bemersyde. They have much in common – these two great sons of
Scotland – but not least have they this – that Time, that great judge
of men, will count them great, not as wielders of pen and sword, but
as great men of character; both ever will be remembered best most
warmly in the hearts of Scots and of those far firth of Scotland, not as
author and Commander-in-Chief, but as great Scottish gentlemen; but
as men, kindly men, gentle men, who loved their God, their country
and their fellowmen. As John Buchan once put it, "Like Sir Walter
Scott, Douglas Haig talked to every man as if he were a blood rela-
tion." They loved the simple things – the wind on the heath, the song
of the birds, the friendly dog, the trusted word of unaffected people,
and their own fireside; and with an integrity of character rooted in
a humble faith, that ever shows the childlike heart without which no
man can ever see God, they treated the two 'imposters" of triumph
and disaster just the same.

Douglas Haig might have become Governor General of Canada;
he preferred to become a Border Laird; he might have been the acting
ruler of millions of unknown people; he preferred to be the active
friend of thousands of his old comrades in arms; he might have been
served by potentates and princes; he preferred to become the servant
of those who had served him. And when he died, still a Field-Marshal
on active service and no less active because it was service of peace, one
member of the Legion he had forged with the straight tools of his own
great character, voiced the feelings of all when he said, "The Legion
has lost a President; but it has gained a Patron Saint."

The old army of the First World War remembers the patron saint;
remembers a Commander-in-Chief who, not content with fighting a
good fight against a common enemy, kept faith with those who had
fought by his side. What they know OF him we only know ABOUT
him. But one thing we know – we know we have here a man of

character. And in the words of his official biographer,[2] "Greatness of character is something different from greatness of mind or of intellect. It is a quality that does not dazzle men, and it is one to which few men of genius, especially those who were also men of action, can lay claim. More often than not, it must be its own reward, for it seldom leads to fame or wealth or power. But when it is possessed by one of those upon whom the searchlight of history beats, it should command the homage of the historian. In moral stature Haig was a giant. It may be easy to find in history a more brilliant man, it would be hard to find a better man. His life was dedicated from the day he left Oxford until the day that he died, to the service of his country, and his reward was the firm faith which the majority of his countrymen reposed in so loyal a servant."

Courage, comradeship, unselfishness, self-sacrifice . . . these are not the prerogatives of war. They are the privileges of life.

Sir Winston Churchill has written that the message of Haig was contained in words he once heard him utter, "A sincere desire to engage the enemy": and the enemy is still as real in peace as any in war: the enemy of covetousness, of selfishness, the enemy of hatred and of callous indifference.

Of the many stories that could be told of Douglas Haig in peace or war there is one which I always feel stands out above all others, showing the genuine greatness of the man. When at the end of the Great War the whole country was rejoicing in final victory, and while men were being honoured and rewarded, praised and thanked, there sat alone in his house in Queen Anne's Gate, London, one man who had received no thanks, who had been given no rewards, who was unhonoured. From his house he could see the cheering crowds roaring almost hysterical enthusiasm as the various heroes passed by. For the last few years he had been probably one of the most hated men in Britain. He had been insulted in the streets and even at times his house had to be protected by the police, and his servants warned to be careful whom they admitted. The reason for all this was because he had said that he was a lover of German philosophy. So this lonely man sat alone while outside the crowds cheered and when evening came and the cheering was dying down his servant entered the room and told him that there was an officer downstairs in uniform and that this officer would like to see him. As the officer had given no name he

[2] Duff Cooper, Lord Norwich.

hesitated to let him in. Then Lord Haldane told the servant to show
the officer up and Haig walked into the room and saluted him. Haig
did not say much, he seldom did; and he didn't stay long. A short
time later he brought Haldane a copy of his *War Dispatches*. After he
had left, Lord Haldane opened the book and saw written inside it, "To
the greatest Secretary of State for War Britain ever had."

I shall never forget the night that his body was brought home to
the Scottish Capital – or rather the early hours of that morning of 4th
February 1928. It was a bleak night, as bleak as a February night in
Edinburgh can be, and the hour was that when normally most folk lay
asleep in bed; but it seemed as though the whole of Edinburgh had
turned out to pay their respects to their own great citizen of whom it
had been written that, though in history it may be easy to find a more
brilliant man, it would be hard to find a better man. It was not only
pride but love that brought them there. How silent that tremendous
crowd who lined the streets was, so silent that you could hear the
clatter of the horses hoofs coming nearer and nearer and hats were
raised and heads were bowed. And they carried his mortal remains
into St. Giles' and thousands passed by in queues four deep on that
cold, wet February day, to pay their last tribute. And the next day the
body of him who could have been buried in St. Paul's Cathedral, was
borne on a simple farm cart from the little border town of St. Boswells
to Dryburgh – a journey of five miles in the country of the Tweed
seltered by the Eildon Hills. So was the great Calvary officer laid to
rest beside the man who once said of himself that he had always a
troop of horses galloping through his brain – Walter Scott.

And in that quiet place amid the green and friendly places he
loved, old comrades in arms meet each year in June in the Scottish
Borders at Dryburgh to remember their task; there are now many
gaps in the ranks; gaps reminding them of comrades that march in the
sunlight of the hill tops while we plod along in the valley below.
Surely it was not for nothing that these gaps are here?

> How can it be in vain, your morning sleeping,
> You who have died for all you loved so much?
> Grassland, and grain that ripened in your keeping,
> Slow patient beasts that knew your gentle touch.
>
> The sprawling farmhouse, white of wall, thatch crested,
> From which you ran with morning in your eyes,

Hay newly-mown, on which at noon you rested,
Watching white clouds adrift in summer skies.

Rain-heavy earth you ploughed in long straight furrows,
Carts, turnip-laden, jolting in the ruts,
Gorse, and the rabbits scuttling to their burrows,
Small winding lanes you searched for autumn nuts.

Woodland and hill, green-tipped by Spring's returning,
Witness of foam upon the cherry trees,
Cold winter evenings, with the great logs burning,
Your sheepdog with his head upon your knees.

Sunrise to sunset, sowing, tending, reaping,
Then dreamless resting at the pillow's touch –
You have not died in vain, who died in keeping
Freedom for all the things you loved so much.[3]

They did not die in vain fighting in war, nor did Haig die in vain
fighting in peace. And you cannot bury a man's spirit. He knew that
in this fight too "every position must be held . . . to the last man; there
must be no retirement. With our backs to the wall and believing in
the justice of our cause, each of us must fight to the end."

James K. Dalgleish
(1919–1942)

When I was a very young man and had just left school I tried to run a
Boys' Club in the Royal Mile of Edinburgh; and "as a recreation" I've
been trying to do it ever since.[4]

In those days you opened the door and hoped for the best – and
sometimes I'm glad to say the worst came too. Then after a while we
had to close the doors; and there, within that room in the Royal Mile
(for we had only a room to start with) was the beginning of a family
(for that, after all, is what any Boys' Club should be). These were the

[3] Mrs. B. R. Gibbs.   [4] See *Our Club* by the author.

days of unemployment and much poverty and little pocket money and few entertainments; but, as in war, hardships knit people together, there was much laughter and a great deal of courage. Having little themselves they were gloriously generous for the little they had they shared royally. At fourteen the boys would scan the evening papers for a job – any old job; and many, too many, landed on dead end jobs which at the insurable age of sixteen they had to leave and join the weary queue for work with their fathers. It wasn't always so easy running the Club; it meant six nights a week and there were times when one wondered whether it was all much use. But as the friendships grew with its happy loyalties and infectious faith not all the disappointments that came could make it of all things most worth while. And of all the boys none stood out more than Jimmie.

When I started the Club I wasn't much older than the oldest (by the way some talked you would have thought I had been in the Crimean War) though I didn't think it wise to give that away! But they did get to know my birthday and it happened to be Jimmie's birthday too; and when he was about eleven he said one evening to me, "My birthday and your birthday are the same; that ought to make us specially good friends shouldn't it?" And "specially good friends" we remained to the end. And when things went wrong Jimmie was there to help to put them right again, and when people were difficult (and people can be difficult you know, bless them) Jimmie was there to cheer me up. And when chaps grumbled a bit and thought I was a bit hard on them, Jimmie was there to explain. I taught him to swim and not many years later he got a life saving medal and swam for the British Boys' Team at the Olympic games in Berlin (there are still some who wait for the prospect of a Life Saving Medal whenever they see me start to go into the water!). He took up running and became for two years the sports champion of the Edinburgh Boys' Clubs; from football in the street closes he played for the Junior Club Football team which, Saturday by Saturday, lost match after match but stuck together until it became the Senior team and lost only one match in its last two years (in running and football too he was in the Boys' Olympic Teams at Berlin); he was confirmed at sixteen and became one of the first to go with Dr George McLeod at the very beginning of the Iona Community; and when he joined the Royal Artillery as a regular soldier and got into the Royal Horse Artillery, though he had never boxed before he won the boxing cup at Wool-

wich; as a young Sergeant he won the Military Medal at Dunkirk —
and how shy he was about it.

On the summer's night on which he was killed he had just done a
broadcast with me; and we'd walked up the river talking, in the midst
of war, of good days in peace in Club and Camp, of the future and of
friends. Tomorrow we were to leave early, first to see off his recently
married wife in London, then each to rejoin our units. But that
tomorrow never came. As our walk ended the sun of that lovely
summer evening was setting. "Good night, sir," he said, "I'll see you
in the morning," and as he turned the corner of the road he looked
round and smiled and with a wave of his hand he called out "See you
in the morning". He was killed that night by enemy action.

And in our camp by the sea on what we call Memorial Hill there
stands a cross and looking across the shore to the East where each new
morning breaks and beneath it, on a cairn of stones placed by a new
generation of boys, carved in stone, his name — Jimmie Dalgleish —
and the names of others, his friends and mine who too gave their lives
that others too may love all that they had loved, and underneath the
words "When the morning was now come they saw Jesus standing on
the shore". And as we remember them in peace as those of you too
remember those you love, we look unto Him who safely keeps them
and with a new day before us we lift up our hearts.

Seven School Sermons

It has been difficult to choose seven since I have preached at many different Schools and Colleges. A selection of School Sermons was published in 1967 by the Oxford University Press under the title of Take Up God's Armour *and since then I have preached many more, all at Fettes College and Loretto School and some at the Edinburgh Academy, Cargilfield, and Clifton Hall. Those chosen here were first preached at The Dragon School, Eton College, Glenalmond, Gordonstoun, Lancing, Oundle, Roedean, Rugby, Sedbergh, Sherborne, Shrewsbury, Stowe, Wellington College, Winchester College, and Uppingham. "A Gentleman's Promise" was first preached before H.M. the Queen and all the Royal Family at Crathie when I was Moderator.*

The Loaf and the Rose

Where there is no vision the people get out of hand.
                              Proverbs 29: 18 (Jerusalem Bible)

or

Where there is ignorance of God the people run wild.
                              Proverbs 29: 18 (The Living Bible)

I came across an old Chinese proverb the other day which says, "If you have only two pennies left spend one on a loaf and one on a rose. The loaf will give life, the rose the reason for living."

Surely it is that lack of the reason for living; that lack of vision (which the Living Bible translates as "ignorance of God") that makes people not "perish" as the Authorised Version puts it, but "get out of hand". For if we are to "see life steadily and see it whole" we must not only live but also see the reason for living.

How thankful we *ought* to be to realise that life does not merely consist in the amount of money we earn or the things we possess, but can realise that, "enough is enough" – provided of course it *is* enough.

It doesn't worry me in the slightest that there are people in their teens who receive now far more money than I ever had; what does worry me is that some of them are not content with that and are always wanting more; for that I am afraid is so often the case.

May I remind you of some of the words of St. Paul that I so often find I am reminding myself of in these days: "godliness with *contentment* is great gain; for we brought nothing into this world and it is certain we carry nothing out" (except of course our own immortal souls).

Now today we are facing quite often very hard times; or what to us appear as very hard times (though, for what I have seen in India

and the Middle and Far East even the poorest here are rich in com-
parison); and as the weeks and possibly months go by they might very
well become even harder. Life isn't always very easy and we haven't
always helped to make it any easier, though it is very much easier than
it was when I first came to my Parish in the Royal Mile. Those of us
who are a bit older know too what hard times can be like, and how
so often they can bring out the best in people so long as we are all in
it together. Look today at the discipline,[1] courage, cheerfulness and
compassion of our troops, not least today in Ireland. Some time ago
there was a really splendid series on Independent Television called
"The World at War". It helped us all, I hope, to see the kind of things
so many of us older people and so many of the present generation's
fathers and grandfathers had to put up with and what they had to
come through; how they met triumph and disaster and treated these
two "impostors" just the same. In all the horror and suffering, men
and women knew at least what comradeship meant and compassion to
those in greater need than themselves – for the tired man helped the
man more tired, the hungry man helped the man more hungry, and
broke bread with him; and each man carried his own pack or was not
too selfish to help another or too proud to be helped by a comrade.
And if some of you think this is fanciful nonsense go back and read
about it again for yourself.

And what made men face these privations, rationing, sacrifices,
and even the supreme sacrifice?

Though the word would not be used or perhaps even the thought
of it would have seemed fanciful, it was vision:

> There'll be bluebirds over
> The white cliffs of Dover
> Tomorrow – just you wait and see.
> There will be joy and laughter
> And peace ever after
> Tomorrow – just you wait and see.

"Tomorrow" – vision. "Peace" – vision. Or even Vera Lynn singing
to the so-called forgotten Army in Burma:

> It's a lovely day tomorrow
> Tomorrow is a lovely day.

"Tomorrow" – vision.

[1] My beloved former General, Sir Neil Ritchie, once defined "discipline", in a
word, as unselfishness – and surely, a most appropriate definition for these days.

And to so many faith either came or returned – faith in God, faith in their fellow-men. In these days, there are no atheists in a trench or a dugout, in stormy waters by sea or perilous jump by air.

But soon, once the corporate effort was over, the vision went. True, a so-called affluent society appeared, for which we all ought to have been grateful. But something went wrong; so many no longer seemed to want to help their neighbour; you must be one up on your neighbour; you don't want enough, you want more than enough; you don't help the man with his burden, you try to lighten your own, and it doesn't matter if his burden becomes heavier; you cannot serve God and Mammon (which is just another word for money) and so you serve Mammon.

"Where there is no vision, the people get out of hand".

And isn't that where so often we find ourselves standing today; need has given way to greed and the first casualty in every crisis is the Ten Commandments and the Two: The Ten Commandments and, if you like, the Eleventh – "a new Commandment I give you, that you love one another".

Yet even in these grim days there is always a brighter side; and if we as Christian people do not show and example who will? There are – or will be perhaps – many folk very much worse off than ourselves; we can help to ease their burden however heavy it may be; there are many more tired, more lonely, more hungry than we are.

After spending two years in the jungle with the Chindits – two years of privation almost unbelievable in their hardship – a vicious enemy, terrible jungle, mountains to climb only to find other mountains still to climb, rivers to cross – with only good comradeship, faith in God and the ultimate vision of peaceful days ahead as his guide, Sir Bernard Fergusson, now Lord Ballantrae, wrote, "One has always read and heard how, when things are really bad, people show up well; and I am glad to be able to say from my own experience that this is perfectly true. When things are only fairly fairly bad men grumble like anything, but when they are appalling they begin to show themselves heroes."

Well we are fairly often at the grumbling bit and I doubt if we ever reach the heroic stage of the Chindits. At least as Christian people let us go forward with an infectious faith and courage and vision – "a lovely day tomorrow" – but only lovely if it is the Way of Him who is the Way, the Truth and the Life; the vision that leads to a love of God, not Mammon. O yes, we need that loaf of bread that we may live; but go too and get yourself a rose to know the reason for living.

Tell . . . Peter

> For he that wavereth is like a wave of the sea driven with the winds and tossed . . . a double minded man is unstable in all his ways.
>
> Epistle to St. James 1: 6ff
>
> Tell . . . Peter.
>
> St. Mark 16: 7

There is a story,[2] though I cannot vouch for its historical accuracy, that when King James I of England and VI of Scotland made a short return visit to Edinburgh, having left Holyroodhouse for London some years before, to try to foist his ecclesiastical views on some unwilling Scottish subjects, he attended the High Kirk of Edinburgh for morning worship on the Sunday. When the Minister rose to preach, this was the text that he gave, staring straight at the King: "James I and VI following: 'For he that wavereth is like a wave of the sea driven with the winds and tossed . . . a double minded man is unstable in all his ways.' 'James I and VI;'"; and the King was "not amused"!

This Letter nearly didn't get into the New Testament at all, even though it is reputed to have been written by the "brother" of our Lord. It was very much disliked by Martin Luther who called it, "an epistle of straw". But we can learn much from this epistle, and I wish that more people would read and study it. Surely St. James is right when he said that unless we show our faith by our works our faith is not worth anything to us.

For one thing, it helps to make us examine ourselves a bit. For it is difficult to know what sort of person each one of us is. In fact we are

[2] I first heard this story from the late Dr Melville Dinwiddie, former Head of the B.B.C. Scotland, who had heard it first from Lord MacLeod of Fuinary.

really, each of us (unless we have become completely settled in life) more than one person.

I am reminded of this every time I show some visitors round the beautifully restored Chessel's Court in the parish of the Canongate; for it was in Chessel's Court that Deacon Brodie was captured robbing the Excise. Now Deacon Brodie was a very respectable citizen of Edinburgh, and you know how very respectable the very respectable city of Edinburgh has always been! He was the kind of man that "nice" people always asked to their house to show how respectable they were too. But what people didn't know was that he was really two quite different people – the very respectable citizen and – well nothing less than a common or garden burglar. You see what he used to do was this: he used to go and visit people and take with him an apprentice; and, while he was seeing the people, the apprentice would wait in the hall or somewhere like that and quietly take a cast of the key, and then when they got home they made a copy of the key and would rob the house during the night. But of course nobody suspected Deacon Brodie. Indeed he would go round and say he was so sorry to hear they had been robbed, while he had done it all the time himself. Fortunately he was caught, to everyone's surprise, red-handed robbing the Excise in Chessel's Court, in the house that still stands there. And it was the story of Deacon Brodie, it is said, that gave Robert Louis Stevenson the idea of writing his famous story of Dr Jekyll – a decent respectable fellow – and Mr Hyde, the unpleasant fellow he sometimes became, and whom he eventually wholly became. He played fast and loose with his two selves so often; and what he thought was the hidden self eventually won, and crushed out the real man that he was.

And I was reminded too of a certain evening at Pirbright Camp when, along with a Padre of the Scots Guards, we went to see a film of Dr Jekyll and Mr Hyde which starred the late Spencer Tracy; and the day after the film I sat with the Scots Guards at their Padre's Hour and the question of the film which we had all seen cropped up. "Was it true to life or exaggerated?" "Which latterly was the real fellow?" "Could the same body turn into two such distinct people?" And so on. It wasn't really a very serious discussion until one fellow said, "We're all like that really." We knew what he meant, and we all of us felt he was right.

It may not be deliberate – it seldom is. Quite small things can make us change our moods and almost ourselves completely.

I remember once during the years of the Second World War waiting with a lot of troops as a part of an audience to listen to a great orchestra playing. It was going to be broadcast and we arrived, as usual, far too soon; and while the troops were waiting I said to the conductor, "I wonder if you would mind just doing two things out of interest, while we are waiting, to keep the troops occupied. Would you first of all play the Solemn Melody by Walford Davies?" He gladly agreed to do this and you never saw such a quiet body of men — there must have been about 800 of them — quiet, peaceful, looking up with great solemnity throughout the whole beautiful passage. Then when it was over I said to the conductor, "Now I wonder if you would play something else just for a few minutes because we have still got another quarter of an hour". At that time there was a very popular tune known as "Tiger Rag" — "I wonder if you would play Tiger Rag?" Now this was a very lively boisterous jazz tune and as he played it that very quiet, peaceful, audience suddenly became almost a screaming mob. They stamped, they clapped their hands, they shouted. Here they were, exactly the same people, and yet within a couple of minutes they had seemingly become totally different. Now what made them change their mood? Quite simply the music. They were the same people but there was something that made them in a very real sense quite different people, and it was music that had done it. Or take the difference that places make to us; we're not the same round our own fireside often as we are round the fireside of other people: we are not the same with one set of people as we are, say, with the folk at home — people, company, environment, all make a difference too. It need not be a difference between good and bad however. The main point is that music, places and people all help to make us different; until sometimes, if you think of it at all, we begin to think and wonder which is the real person.

You may remember how the young Cosmo Lang, son of the Moderator of the General Assembly of the Church of Scotland, and reading Law at Oxford, became a member of the Church of England and later became Archbishop of Canterbury. One of the first things he did when he went over to the Church of England was to attend a Conference of young Anglicans taken by the good Bishop of Lincoln, Edward King. He arrived late for the Conference and found them all kneeling at prayer and felt very embarrassed. Bishop King leaned over to him and smiled and said, "Don't worry, we ain't as good as we looks." Well none of us are "as good as we looks", especially when we are in Church or School Chapel. In all our changing moods, which is the "you" you picture yourself to be, the "you" you hope you really are? Are you what folk think you are or what your best friend thinks you are? Or are you even what you think you are yourself? Did you say, "God knows"? You're quite right – God knows, and He's the only one who does; though we each have a good idea.

And other people too have an idea. "Bill's changed a lot," they say; and by that they mean he's getting more considerate, or getting more callous; he's looking so much fitter, or he is looking a bit under the weather. Change is usually so gradual when you're living with people; but its so very noticeable when you've been parted for a bit. Look, for example, how much the baby's grown, how much more comfortable your room looks, how fresh the old street seems – living with it all you didn't notice it. And change of character is more obvious too when folk meet after separation. Either the Jekyll or the Hyde is winning. The tragedy is that no one really wants the Hyde to win, least of all the fellow himself. Still, in his better moments, he's his real self. Look at the excuses we make for the Hyde in us! "After all, I . . ." "It won't happen again, but you know, a chap . . ." and so on. Excuses as old as Adam – literally as old as Adam . . . look up Genesis 3: 12 if you don't follow me. Only Adam was a bit of an ass – he made the excuses to God. We're too clever for that – we make them to human beings instead, and sometimes we take them in – other times we only think we do! And they, bless their hearts, so often pretend they believe us. For folk don't like to think we are what we don't like to think we're becoming.

And it's so easy, isn't it? It just begins as "Let's try . . ." or "It doesn't matter once." Remember Jekyll started like that: it was to be "an interesting experiment", that was all. But it so often leads to more. "We want to try the experiment once", that's how it's sometimes put. But do remember that experence is nearly always "what we get when looking for something else". And its usually when we don't know what it is that we're looking for that we make a mess of life. "Let a man strive to his uttermost for his life's set prize," said Sir Ernest Shackleton once; and if ever a man strove to the uttermost it was he. What is your life's set prize? A good conscience before God and your fellow men – and your home? A good and happy memory to leave behind? Whatever it is, if it is worth striving for – let's strive for it. And believe me, we'll never begin to touch it if we let the Jekyll think it can be hidden in the Hyde.

It isn't easy – that bit – it isn't easy. If it were easy, there would be no such thing as character. There's a bit of the beast in every man, and character is the victory over the beast. The "good and the great" have always "battled with fate", and won through; but they have never been able to do it in their own strength.

I remember getting a letter from a Guardsman who was a former member of my Boy's Club who had been for some time fighting in the Desert war. "I've seen a bit of life," he said, "these last four years. When I left the Club I thought I was a real man of the world, but I hadn't seen anything yet: but, sir, one thing I can promise you, I've never let you down." But then he sees to it that he gets to a service some time every week, and he says his prayers somewhere and at some time every day. I only hoped that I hadn't let *him* down too badly.

There is a very lovely book written by a former Earl of Lytton about his own son who was killed in an air accident. The book is called *Anthony*. In it there is a letter from his son to him when he was appointed Viceroy of India. The boy had to stay at home and go to school. This is a part of what he wrote, "Oh I wish you all the most excellent things and I pray I may be worthy of you while you are away." That is surely what we all hope and pray when we are our real selves; that we will not let other folk down who love us, and that we will prove worthy of them and so bring happiness to them and happiness to ourselves, and so begin to find our real selves, the folk God wants us to be.

I remember once when Captain John Ridgway who had just rowed across the Atlantic with Sergeant Chay Blyth, was lunching at my Manse shortly after they had made that remarkable crossing – because neither of them had been oarsmen before – a friend of mine said to him, "Would you do it again?", and added, laughing, "I suppose you have been asked that question dozens of times since you got back." And he replied, "No, as a matter of fact I have not been asked that question before except last week when the Queen asked me." And my friend said to him, "And what did you say to the Queen?" And Captain Ridgway replied, "I said to the Queen, 'I would do it again for you Ma'am.'"

Well it is wonderful what people will do and do again, however hard, for those they respect or love, isn't it? And whatever mess we have made or are making of our lives, we have always got another chance.

You remember the story of the disciple called Peter. He was perfectly sure of himself. He would never betray his Master. But he did, you remember. "I don't even know Him," he said; and then you remember what happened some days later after that most tremendous event in history, the Resurrection of that same Master. "Go and tell the disciples – and Peter." "And Peter" – you see, the Lord of all good life was ready to start afresh in the morning, and especially with the man who had denied Him. And He is always willing to start afresh in the morning.

One Thing you Lack

And Jesus looking upon him loved him.

St. Mark 10: 21

The rich young ruler[3] had three great qualities – wealth, health and authority.

He had riches – a lot of money: yet there is a richness in life that has got nothing to do with money. He was young with all the vision, the confidence, the opportunities that youth offers. Yet all can be as young as they feel. (I remember once Lord Baden-Powell when he was 75 years old saying to me as he watched some 15-year-old Scouts looking rather too serious and important, "I often feel that I am younger than some of my youngest Scouts!") He had authority – he was a ruler. But that can lead either to dictatorship or to leadership, and leadership can be dangerous if not leading the right way.

This young man seemed to have the best of all these qualities but yet there was something missing. With these three great qualities a rich young ruler could be a bumptious promiscuous bounder, but this man we read had lived a decent life – clean and honest – "all these

[3] St. Mark 10: 17–22.

things have I kept from my youth up". But not even his goodness of character had brought him a complete inner peace. He was eager and ready to confide in Jesus. He had the makings of a disciple.

One thing hindered him – in his case his wealth. And Jesus boldly and unhesitatingly asked the young man to stop prizing so highly and holding on to the one thing that was keeping his back, and asked him to come with Him. Jesus wants the man, not his money.

Now this came as rather a shock to the disciples because their idea of the Kingdom of Heaven was bound up with politics and economics (as so many people's idea of the Kingdom of Heaven seems to be today).

To obtain eternal life – which was what he asked for – he was told that he must be prepared to pay the cost, which all the money in the world couldn't buy – there must be an undivided allegiance to God.

But let's be clear: Jesus doesn't regard wealth as an evil in itself. It is a possible evil, and here it seems an actual evil. A man to whom money has been his chief end in life is in a desperate state. That applies not only to the rich who make riches their aim; it applies just as much to the covetous who either envy the rich or seek riches as an end in itself. The Commandment "Thou shalt not covet" includes nearly all the others.

Now I want you to notice the eagerness of the young man; "he ran to Him"; and I want you to notice his reverence – "he knelt to Him"; and notice too that real earnestness of his question. This was the kind of man he was – eager, earnest and reverent. I wonder how many of us would run and kneel and ask how we could inherit eternal life, than which there can surely be few more important questions in all the world.

Jesus probes the man's needs rather than answers his question. This man says he has kept all the Commandments. You see the point? To avoid the obvious sins is a poor form of doing right. A full life is larger than just "not doing" certain things. Are you content with doing people no wrong? But is there no good you can do them? You have not killed anyone – but have you enlarged anyone's life – helped him to live as he ought? You have not stolen – but have you added to his store? You have not said bad things about him – but have you said any good things? You have brought no sorrow to him – but have you brought him happiness? . . . You see the point?

Mere respectability consists largely in not doing things: Christianity adds "in doing things". And that is where the rich young ruler failed, and where so many of us fail too. We may not have done in this life much harm, but what good have we done?

In ordinary life we only ask great things of those we love. We never ask or expect from those we really love the "second-best"; we expect the best, however weak that best may be. I remember once somebody saying to me that I expected too much of the boys in my Boys' Club. Well, I got them together and told them this and said, "Well in future would you like me to expect the second-best from you; I am sure you wouldn't." No one could be expected to do more than his best and certainly nobody can be expected to do less, if we really love and trust them.

And Jesus because he loved the young man asks one great thing of him.

Now note this: Jesus never demanded the surrender of wealth from all men who would be his disciples, nor would he tell this man to give his wealth to the poor if material possessions, things to be given, were in themselves evil. But he knows what is keeping *this particular man* back. And the question he puts to the rich young ruler is not to throw away all his money — that would be foolish — but "with all you have, with your great wealth, with all you could give away, what real good could you do to others, indeed have you done to others? How much have you really tried to help and comfort and give strength to others as you might and could have done?"

Some of the things that keep *us* back may be harmless in themselves and differ with each one of us. "You must leave father and mother", said He who told us to "honour our father and mother"; "You must give up certain friendships" said He who consecrated human friendship by His love for St. John. You may have to give up something in *itself* not bad because in your case (or in mine) it holds you back. Love of beauty is a glorious thing; but it might lead us the wrong way:

> Pray! Have I prayed!
> When I am worn with all my praying!
> When I have bored the blessed angels
>   with my battery of prayers!
> It's the proper thing to say, but it's
>   only saying, saying,

And I cannot get to Jesus for the
      glory of her hair.[4]

Now note that "the glory of her hair" was a lovely thing, but in this particular case it was a stumbling block. It needn't be to others. In Lord Wavell's Anthology called *Other Men's Flowers* there is this rather lovely verse called "Blondie goes to Heaven":

      Paul said, and Peter said,
      And all the Saints alive and dead
      Swore she had the sweetest head
      Of yellow, yellow hair.

The rich young ruler found the demand at first too hard, but he is sad for he knows he is throwing away his chance of life. Here is the tragedy of life — a man refuses his own chief good because he cannot face the cost of obtaining it.

So the story of the rich young ruler tells us to cease feeling that moral responsibility is enough — *not* doing things. It isn't enough. Goodness doesn't just consist in *not* doing things. We must take all we have and are and spend ourselves and all we have on others too and use whatever gifts we have however small. That is the way to begin to find true happiness. That is the way we can begin to find out how we can inherit eternal life.

Now there is a happy sequel to the story. Tradition — and never scorn tradition — says that the rich young ruler was none other than St. Mark himself; and St. Mark, you may remember, travelled with St. Paul on some of his journeys and became the first Bishop of the great Church at Alexandria. So you see, there was still a chance and he must have taken it.

Oh yes, "I'm quite a respectable fellow; I try to keep the Commandments; I don't do this and I don't do that". That is not enough. "One thing you lack." Just as we are He looks on us and yet still loves us.

But may God never have to look on us with the sorrow of one looking on a loved one who has refused to be what he might have been, and could have been.

                    [4] G. A. Studdert Kennedy.

A Little While

A little while, and you will see me no more; again a little
while and you will see me.
They said "What does He mean by 'a little while'? We do
not know what He means."
Jesus knew that they were wanting to ask Him.
St. John 16: 16, 18, 19 (R.S.V.)

There are passages read from the Bible which are very difficult to
follow sometimes without explanation or commentary, and at first
sight this is one of them.

What is this "a little while"?

Well not even the disciples knew: "What is this? What is He talk-
in about? I wish we knew." And Jesus knew that they wanted to ask
Him.

Now there are lots of things we cannot understand in this world
and many things we will never fully understand. If faith is only what
we understand then it isn't faith. In this "little while" we call life, or
part of life, we cannot always understand the mystery of pain or
suffering or the apparent triumph of evil over good: but only for a
little while; then in a little while we shall.

Then too there are lots of things we did not once understand, but
understand better now perhaps as we look back on them. Why some
things happened in the way they did, in a way we sometimes did not
understand, or did not want, and yet how often our "little while"
disappointments become God's appointments.

There are lots of things that even the disciples at the time could
not understand but that we can, or should, understand – just as they
understood later. The disciples did not understand why their Master
should be crucified; but that was before they had experienced the
Easter message.

For with faith goes patience: a "little while" is not *never* or
forever.

There is a sense in which our life on earth is just, compared with
eternity, a very little while. No one is alive now who sat here a
hundred years ago; and in a hundred year's time no one here will be
living on this earth, and many who will sit where you now sit are not

yet born. Compared with eternity, our loved ones too are here with us "a little while"; and we sometimes forget that not one of us is here for ever and few for very long as time goes.

You may remember how Edmund Gosse wrote:

Last night I woke and found between us drawn –
Between us where no mortal fear may creep –
The vision of Death dividing us in sleep;
And suddenly I thought, ere light shall dawn
Some day – the substance, not the shadow, of Death
Shall cleave us like a sword. The vision passed,
But all its new-born horror held me fast,
And till day broke I listened for your breath.
Some day to wake, and find that coloured skies
And piping in the woods, and petals wet,
Are things for aching memory to forget;
And that your living hands and mouth and eyes
Are part of all the world's old histories!
Dear God! A little longer, ah not yet!

"A little longer, ah not yet." A *little* longer. But our faith as Christians tells us that one day we shall see each other again – "a little while you shall see me and then a little while you shall not see me". "A little while" – not "forever"; we are not here forever but for a little while. We have not parted from sight forever but – for a little while.

Then, again, there is this time of perplexity: "We do not know what He means." What is it all about? We all have times of "do not know", and it is good that we do not know all the answers all the time. As Joseph Parker of the City Temple once put it – "We want to know enough that we may pray in a humble tone." There are parts of the Bible we can hardly read – well then, leave them alone for the time being; there are some passages which we can only partially explain and we can go to them now and again to see if the buds are beginning to open; and there are passages which are only too clear, ever clear to us since they were first read at our mother's knee. These are the most difficult. May I quote again to you Mark Twain's words: "Some people are worried about the passages of the Bible they cannot understand – what worries me are the bits I *can* understand."

People so often make excuses that they "cannot understand" – and that is often true – but there is so much we *can* understand and that is enough in the lifetime of most men and women; and so we must be careful in case we make a time of perplexity a time of excuse. Of course, as I have said, there is much in this "little while" we call life that we cannot understand but again in "a little while" it shall be made clear to us. That is a part of our Resurrection Faith.

Our Lord never rebuked those in perplexity: "Why do you worry so, oh you of little faith." It was a kindly comfort, not a stern rebuke: "What you don't understand now you will understand later – have patience." We cannot do everything, learn everything, know everything, in this small span, this "little while", we call life.

Jesus did not rebuke the disciples' perplexity; He said, "What you know not now you shall know hereafter; hereafter you shall see, hereafter you shall know." There is sometimes a discipline in bewilderment and a discipline of bewilderment. We have not lost our faith when at all times we cannot explain it. "We cannot understand all this," said the disciples: sometimes all was clear, sometimes all was baffling. "What is this that He says – 'a little while'?" They could not tell what He said. But after a little while they gloriously knew. And if we too are sometimes lost it is in an infinite ocean of truth and love: lost, if you like, "in wonder, love and praise".

Yes, there is discipline in bewilderment. Many think religion consists of clear views, but what chances are there of clear views in cloudy and grey days and times of unrest to the soul, and sadness and hopelessness because the last door we battered at did not open? Our view is not always clear – but the way is. What was it Browning said?

> . . . I remember well
> One journey, how I feared the track was missed,
> So long the city I desired to reach
> Lay hid; when suddenly its spires afar
> Flashed through the circling clouds; you may conceive
> My transport; soon the vapours closed again,
> But I had seen the city. . . .

And he knows the questions we would like to ask, how many and how urgent.

He finds us sitting by the grave and He knows we are desirous to ask Him. "A little while" – hereafter.

He knows that we are "wanting to ask Him" why so often the man who never prays would seem to prosper, and in the garden of the man of faith so little seems to grow compared with that of him who has no faith. "A little while" – hereafter. Oh there are so many things we would desire to ask Him. Yet our very desire to ask is a proof of the existence of our faith. Our very perplexities are a part of the evidence of our faith. Without faith and love we would never care to ask questions of this strange world we live in. The Bishop of Southwark tells how a few months after he became a bishop in 1959 he met Dr Donald Coggan, the present Archbishop of Canterbury, in Cambridge as he was about to return to his diocese to take the funeral service of a brilliant young man whom he admired.

"Donald", he said, "do experiences like this ever make you question your belief in the existence of God?"

"Of course they do", he answered, "but that is what faith and love are all about."

Patience and self-control, and trying to live this short span we call life faithfully and trustfully and kindly – that is what He asks of us. After all, even at its longest it is only "a little while". Then there is "hereafter" when the day breaks and the shadows flee away and "lost in wonder, love and praise" we shall ask no questions then.

The Resurrection

If Christ be not risen, then is our preaching vain, and your faith is also vain.

I Corinthians 15: 14

To me it has always been one of the most comforting things of our faith, and one of the surest evidences among many, of the truth of the New Testament, that doubts and difficulties are quite frankly stated – "but some doubted", we read, and "after that many of His disciples followed Him no more," and so on. To doubt is quite natural. But we are wrong not to doubt our doubts sometimes. Common sense is all right – though it is not as common as it might be! – but for a thing to be sense, it needn't necessarily be common. George Romanes, who was a famous Professor of Physics at Oxford, in the days when he was an agnostic, wrote three essays attacking Christianity; later through the influence of Bishop Gore he changed, and wrote against his own former views. And there he says quite openly, writing now as a Christian – that so much of the Christian faith is opposed to common sense. "No doubt," he writes, "utterly so; but so it *ought* to be *if true*. Common sense," he went on, "is merely a rough requisite of common experience; but the Birth and Resurrection of our Lord, whatever else it may have been, cannot have been a common event."

And so I feel it is good and rather comforting to find that one of our Lord's own closest friends, St. Thomas, felt about the Resurrection story – the story of the first Easter – what a lot of good men and women feel today – felt it hard to believe. But, he did not leave the fellowship because of that; he stuck by the others who did believe; and that's very important. He stayed with them; and in the end of the day he died a martyr's death near Madras in India, on a little spot still called the Mound of St. Thomas which I visited a few years ago. His faith must have been pretty sound by that time; he must have been convinced; he died a martyr's death for it. You must believe most strongly in a thing when you are prepared to die for it, mustn't you? (And incidentally, what are the things you would die for rather than betray?)

You see, they didn't expect to see our Lord again, although He'd told them. He was "crucified, dead, and buried". They had loved Him so much as a friend; but this was really too much to believe. They had respected Him as a leader; but being human folk, they wanted to see "results" as they called it – results – on this earth. They had been mystified by the whole business and just could not understand it now. They were depressed beyond words, and they went back glad with glad memories, but sad because it was now all over.

And then suddenly it all changed, and this is a fact of history – it all changed. And what they'd naturally thought had been the end of a rich experience, they discovered was but the beginning of a richer one. What they had thought was all over now, they discovered had only just begun. Timid men became brave, and cowards became heroes. Yes! men who feared to confess to a servant girl their allegiance to their earthly friend, now stood boldly before governors and kings, risking all – proud of their allegiance to their risen Master.

Before one of these books which we now call the Gospels had been written, we find men betting their whole faith – risking their very lives – on the truth of the Resurrection: for the Christian faith is nothing if it is not the faith in, and of, the Resurrection.

It was a man who had not only thought the Resurrection non-sense, but wicked, and who had done his level best to stamp out the belief in it and to persuade those who so believed – it was this man who was later to write – "If Christ be not risen, then is our preaching vain, and your faith is also vain." And St. Paul – for I don't need to tell you that he was the man – knew that there was no "if" about it, for he knew its truth. He knew that this only was sense – that the world was changed from that day.

Try as they could no one could disprove the Resurrection story: with all their learning, with all their cunning, with all their power, their earthly power, there was but one answer to the empty tomb.

Remember this, that not fifty days after the Crucifixion, the Apostles were preaching the Resurrection without fear, and openly, in Jerusalem, of all places; and by their evidence, their courage and their transparent sincerity, convinced thousands. The facts they preached were unchallenged because they were above challenge. Christ was risen indeed. And so a few men, changed in so few days, sounded the first clarion call to the mighty conquest which is still going on. A few timid men, so recently in retreat, had become more than conquerors; and the Christian Church, founded on the Ressurec-tion belief, had gained its conquest and sent forth its first Order of the Day.

"No one," writes one of our distinguished modern preachers, Professor James Stewart, "no one believes that a spiritual movement like the Church, so indestructible in its nature, so illimitable in its possibilities, so indispensable in its value for the souls of men, could ever spring from, or be inspired by, anything which was not utterly and genuinely real . . . only the fact of the Resurrection of Jesus can explain the Church of the living God." Oh, yes, you may not like the Church, but you cannot deny why the Church and that the Church is.

Let us consider just something of the inner meaning of the story. The fact is a fact, and if Christ be not risen from the dead, "then is our preaching vain" and your faith and my faith is also vain. What are some of the things that the Resurrection means to us? I think first it means this: let me put it this way – did you ever, as a small boy, as I often did, dam up a river and change its course? – a small river, of course, dam it up perhaps to make a pond and sail boats on it, or

perhaps even make a raft? By doing that, we were altering the course
of the nature of that river, and as man can alter the course of nature, so
all the more can God alter the course of nature, and never let us forget
that.

The death of Jesus Christ had seemed blasphemous to orthodox
Jews – the Messiah dying as a criminal – and very many decent, good-
living religious people who had just found a new hope and a new faith
in Jesus must have wondered at their own complete disillusionment.
But here in the Resurrection story is God's sudden and quite un-
expected witness and proof of the very highest and most daring hopes
that have ever been cherished about Jesus. Here He sealed, once and
for all, the claim of Jesus, that He was the Son of God and the Saviour
of the world. And if that is not true, then is our preaching vain and
our faith is vain. It also means – this Resurrection story – this story of
Easter Day – that goodness must ultimately triumph.

Jesus had staked all He had and all He was on the absolute worth
of goodness and truth and love. Nothing could make Him move from
this. He did not care how unpopular He became; He did not care how
outspoken He was, and He gave a new meaning to the word happiness. The only thing that really mattered, He told us, was goodness,
and truth, and love – real love – not some sloppy, sentimental version
of it. He had always taught that, and, what is far more important, He
had always lived as He taught; and possibly most important of all, He
died for these things. Now, had our Lord never been raised from the
dead, we could only conclude that these things just didn't matter –
that they were mere delusions and that the whole world was chaotic.
Do you ever really think what a world this would be – what a hopeless world this would be – what an empty world this would be, if God
had nor raised Jesus from the dead? We would never have known for
certain which side the universe itself is on. And on that first Easter
morning God endorsed and countersigned goodness. We know now,
the world knows for all time, that the universe is on the side of all
that is truly good. And so, when Jesus was raised, goodness once and
for all won, and her banner flew, and flies for ever, the right way up,
and at the top of the mast. No one now may stamp out that ultimate
Love:

> So through the clouds of Calvary there shines
> His face, and I believe that Evil dies,
> And Good lives on, loves on, and conquers all –

All war must end in peace. Those clouds are lies.
They cannot last. The blue sky is the truth.
For God is love.
Such is my faith, and such
My reasons for it, and I find them strong
Enough. And you?
You want to argue?
Well,
I can't.
It is a choice. I choose the Christ.[5]

And then I would say that the Resurrection next means that im-
mortality, life after death, is assured. I think it is true to say that the
one thing which struck the old pagan world more than anything else
as they watched those early Christian men at work in the world was
their contempt of death; martyrs going willingly to die unafraid, to
die for their faith, willing to be thrown to the lions for their faith;
Christian men and women everywhere, wherever their faith was true,
waving goodbye as one goes on a journey when death called them.
And it was the goodbye on a journey – never the goodbye for ever.
And it was, and is, the risen Christ who robs that last enemy – Death –
of his power. "I go to prepare a place for you," He had said; and if
death means that, then why fear? The conquest of death by Him in-
volves the conquest of death for us. "Because," He said, "because I
live, you shall live also." And now they knew, and we know, it to be
true. In the words of the old verse – Easter morning brought "immor-
tality to light", and the Christians, seeing death now lying broken,
would shout, just as the Psalmist has shouted long years before, "God
is gone up with a shout, the Lord with the sound of a trumpet."

The last thing I'd like to say here about Easter is just this – that
Christ is alive for evermore. You see, even when later they could no
longer actually see Him, they knew they had not lost Him, and that,
more than anything else, accounted surely for the change in them.
That, more than anything else, surely explains the true greatness of all
those who since then have followed Him. Every day His own words
sounded and they knew by their experience how true it was, "Lo, I
am with you always." Through all their sufferings, in all their happiness, and all the days of their life, it was no fading memory that kept
them up – it was a living presence. He went by their side, and when

[5] G. A. Studdert Kennedy.

death came to them he came as a friend for they knew He still was near them. And such it must be for all God's children everywhere, and this is nothing new – really no new miracle. For if Christ is risen indeed, which means if He is living now, what could be more natural than that He should ever be with His friends? "Lo, I am with you always." Will you remember that? Tonight before you go to bed, and tomorrow morning when you wake us. Such is our faith, and those who believe in Him with all their heart, know it to be true.

In John Masefield's drama, *The Trial of Jesus*, there is a fine passage in which the Roman centurion in command of the soldiers at the Cross comes back to Pilate to hand in his report of the day's work. He gives his report, and then Pilate's wife beckons to the centurion and asks him to tell her how the prisoner died. And when the story has been told by the centurion – "Do you think He is dead?" she suddenly asks him. "No, lady," answers the centurion, "I don't." "Then where is He?" she says. "Let loose in the world, lady, where neither Roman nor Jew can stop His truth."

Nothing In . . . and Nothing Out

> But godliness with contentment is great gain. For we brought nothing into this world, and it is certain we carry nothing out.
> I Timothy 6: 6–7

It was a sad sight to see in Hong Kong harbour the once so beautiful, so famous, *Queen Elizabeth* protruding from the water – a burnt-out, empty ship. As I went round it in a launch I was told the story of a Commander of one of the great Queens who had many a time sailed backwards and forwards across the Atlantic. Whenever he was getting the ship into port he would rush to consult a bit of paper and then go back to give instructions. People wondered what was on the bit of paper. Was it a prayer? Or some sort of complicated diagram? One day somebody looked at the paper, just to see what it really was; and what was written on the paper was simply four words, "Port left, starboard right." You see, it was to him the most obvious thing in the world, and he was frightened he might forget it.

Do you ever think how often it is the most obvious things that we are often most likely to forget. For example, very few Ministers would lead the Lord's Prayer in public without having it written out in front of them. They know it so well and it is so "obvious" — so they might forget it. There are so many things that we take or took for granted because they are or were so obvious. After being kidnapped for eight weeks in the hands of the Quebec Liberation Front terrorists, the British diplomat, Mr James Cross, discovered how much the simple things of life meant to him — the things which he had so often taken for granted. This is what he said:

"One of the things that this dreadful period has given me is a sense of appreciation of the ordinary simple things of life which most people take for granted — the ability to live with one's family, to talk with one's friends, and to breathe fresh air. We take these as normal things and part of our everyday life. We don't put a price on them, but when we are deprived of them we suddenly realise how important they are, and how unimportant other things are."

I always took for granted the food I ate each day until I saw in India starving children; I took for granted a bed to sleep in until I saw men sleeping in the streets and in the station; I took for granted my home until I saw orphans who had never known what a home meant; I took for granted my health until I saw men without fingers or feet and with faces deformed almost beyond recognition in leprosy colonies in, for example, India or in that beautiful Island I visited off Hong Kong with its Chapel called "The Lord is willing".

The people we know best, the people in our own homes, so often we tend to forget them and are so polite to those whom we know far less. We take them for granted until one day they are no longer with us. And so it is often too with the anniversary of a School; we just take our School and we take those who teach us for granted; the folk who sent us there for granted, and all the rest of it — the obvious things that we ought to know best of all, yet the things we have so often got to be reminded of. That is one reason why we have such days as Founder's Days and Anniversaries — just to help to remind us again.

Sometimes it isn't so much that we forget, it is just that we don't like expressing our feelings — perhaps we don't know how to express our feelings. "Warm are our hearts, although we do not bare them," as Neil Munro once put it. Sometimes we in Scotland are particularly bad about this. If after a very enjoyable day you ask somebody if they had really enjoyed it, the answer will probably be that it "wasn't bad" or it was "quite good"; and really all the time what they mean is that they had had a wonderful time. I remember a famous doctor telling me that one Christmas he wanted to give his Ward in the Infirmary a particularly good time. He took a lot of trouble, had the Ward decorated and saw that all had a specially good meal with crackers and entertainment. He really did everything he could to make it a particularly wonderful Christmas time; and next morning as he walked round the various beds he was rather hoping that they would say what a splendid time they had yesterday and "thank you very much" – not that he wanted thanks, but he did want to know that they had enjoyed themselves as he meant them to do. And at last he came to the last bed and rather timidly said to the last patient, "Did you all enjoy yourselves yesterday?" to which the patient replied, "I didn't hear any complaints".

Not that we need to show our appreciation always obviously or even in words. In a certain part of Africa, I've been told, there was a Missionary whose name I don't remember and I don't know if he is even remembered very much, except possibly in the Mission Field which he so faithfully served. He had in the Mission a small boy who used to do the housework, clean the Missionary's shoes, dust the shelves, do some odd sweeping and all that sort of thing. The Missionary saw that this boy had something to him, therefore he tutored him and helped him in every way he could. He sent the boy to School; the boy did very well at School, indeed so well that he won a scholarship and went to the University. He did so well at the University he passed out with a high Honours degree and went later to America where he got a further degree. He came back to his own country of Africa and became Principal of a great College; indeed he became the most famous African of his day. One day this Missionary – whose name I don't remember – received word from this now famous African that he wanted to come back to the old Mission Field and see the Missionary again and see the place where he had been brought up as a boy; and so he arrived in the evening and the Missionary wondered what he would be like, it was too late in the evening to tell because the Missionary was tired and had gone to bed early. Would he be pompous, a bit conceited? Well the Missionary woke up early the next morning, the sun was rising and he had a strange feeling there was someone in his room. He sat up and looked round and at first he could not see anyone, and then he saw somebody but he could not quite see who the person was because his head was bent, and he looked again and he saw that it was this very famous African – the most famous African of his day – cleaning the Missionary's shoes. You see, he had not forgotten and there he was showing his thanks in this wonderful way.

And so we should never forget what can so often seem the obvious, never to become so small that we don't like to show our feelings. Never forget that it is often a sign of strength, not weakness, to show our feelings.

Surely great faith, like great music and great literature, demands a legitimate emotional expression. In the book *The Turn of the Tide* there is one rather moving entry in Lord Alanbrooke's diary. He and Winston Churchill are in Tripoli watching the victorious 51st Division marching past. "They swung by with rhythmic precision, the pipes skirling, the sun glinting on their armour." Alanbrooke, who had seen Britain struggle through for years of serious reverse and dismal defeats, felt a lump rise in his throat and a tear flow down his cheek. A little ashamed, he half-turned his head and saw that Churchill was crying too. These were two strong men. This was a high moment which demanded expression of their deepest feelings too.

And so too let us never forget to give thanks to God (it is worth remembering that the highest form of Christian worship, Holy Communion, is also known as the Eucharist – the giving of thanks) – to thank God "for our creation, preservation and all the blessings of this life, but above all for His inestimable love in the redemption of the world by Our Lord, Jesus Christ, for the means of grace, and for the hope of glory". And let us too always remember that there is much we rightly cannot understand of the greatness, the glory and the splendour of God (rightly understand because, as A. J. Balfour once put it, "A religion that is small enough for our understanding is not great enough for our need"). Our faith is not as complicated as some of us would like to make out. When G. K. Chesterton was quite a young man he once wrote this in his notebook:

There was a Man who lived in the East centuries ago
And now I cannot look at a sheep or a sparrow

A lily or a cornfield, a raven or a sunset
A vineyard or a mountain, without thinking of Him.
If this be not to be Divine, what is it?

I like the story of Collins, the famous freethinker of last century who, while out walking one Sunday morning, met an old ploughman going to Church. Collins asked him where he was going. The old man replied, "To Church, sir." "And what are you going to do there?" asked Collins. "I am going to worship God", said the ploughman. "And pray", said Collins, with a rather superior air, "pray, is your God a great or a little God?" "He is both, sir." "How can he be both?" said Collins – this time rather more surprised than amused. "He is so great", said the ploughman, "that the heaven of heavens cannot contain Him; and so little that He can dwell in my heart." Surely here the ploughman summed up one of the greatest and most profound truths of our faith, the truth of the God who is –

Centre and soul of every sphere,
Yet to each loving heart how near.

Whom so easily we forget until . . .

So in these sometimes greedy and pessimistic days it is good to remember again that "godliness with contentment is great gain", and that "as we brought nothing into this world, it is certain we carry nothing out" – except our immortal souls; yet always remembering, "You shall not see my face, unless your brother is with you."

A Gentleman's Promise

Jesus came up and spoke to them. He said "All authority in heaven and on earth has been given to me. Go therefore and make disciples of all nations . . . and teach them to observe all the commands I gave you. And know that I am with you always; yes to the end of time."

St. Matthew 28: 18 (Jerusalem Bible)

It is a strange phenomenon of human nature that each generation seems to almost rejoice in thinking that it alone has never had it so

bad. Materially, that is fairly good nonsense. One has only got to
know the Royal Mile in Edinburgh to appreciate the vast change for
good that has come in our own generation; and to those who don't
remember the bad old days may I mention and so remind those who
do (for they certainly often need reminding) that when as a schoolboy
and student I first knew the Royal Mile – and later Canongate in
particular – nearly every room was a house, poverty was the order of
the day, men were not only unemployed but often unemployable,
and the only time many saw the country was once a year at the
Sunday school picnic; boys left school at 14 and got odd jobs until the
insurable age of 16 and were then out of work with little prospect of
even unskilled work available; hardly one ever went to a University.
Eight, nine or ten families would share one lavatory and often one
tap, and families lived, were born, died, washed, slept and ate in one
room. And looking even further back to the "good old days" of
churchgoing, as far as my and similarly situated parishes were concerned, they just didn't exist. Let me give you an example that is all
the more pertinent because it illustrates a time when the Canongate
parish was at its utmost capacity in the middle of last century, when a
survey of 411 families showed that only 45 attended any Communion
and 296 were entirely unconnected with any Church, and when
almost exactly 100 years ago Mr McNair came as Minister to Canongate he found that in this parish numbering more than 10,000 people,
the membership had fallen to about 500 and the attendance at Holy
Communion had been as low as under 200.

True, many others went to the local Missions where the clothes
they wore didn't matter so much and where at least they got an assurance that in the hereafter things would be better, that there would be
"pie in the sky when they die", that when the Roll was called up
yonder they would be there, and that there would be "no more
whisky there in my Father's house" (for drunkenness was not the least
of the problems); and the hope of heaven was all the more to be desired often because of the constant reminder of the fear of hell. There
was also a cup of tea and a bun provided.

In the Church at large there were the same problems. If you read
through some of the Reports of the Church during last century and the
beginning of this, once again I read things had never been so bad.
Church-going was poor, money was scarce (I am referring to the Old
Kirk, the Free Kirk may have been a bit different), there was a short-

age of candidates for the Ministry, permissiveness among the young was rampant – called in those days the "Bohemian" life – indeed in such highly "respectable" areas in Edinburgh as Morningside and Newington there were complaints in *The Scotsman* of the unruly behaviour of the young people there. Here is an extract from *The Scotsman* where attention is called to "the disgraceful state of affairs which has prevailed for some time between Nicolson Square and Newington when almost every evening large bands of young men parade the streets ringing people's bells. Within the last month a lady was so abused that she had to be placed under medical treatment and a young man has had his face so disfigured that he had to keep indoors for several days. When the Lord Provost sent for the Superintendent of Police he added that besides these young men, many children of respectable parents influenced by their bad example, had been guilty of like conduct." "They never behaved like that in our days." Didn't they? That's from *The Scotsman* – of March *1867*!

Nor do I need to remind you that all this goes back long before these days or of how in the introductory letter to the Westminster Confession written in 1643, there is a complaint "concerning the decay of the power of godliness, and more especially of the great corruption of youth". "Youth today is rotten to the core" reads a Babylonian statement of 3000 B.C. Or there were those hackneyed words that begin: "the young people of today think of nothing but themselves. They have no reverence to parents and old age. They are impatient of restraint. And as for the girls they are immodest and unwomanly in speech and dress and behaviour." And *that* was written in 1294 by Peter the Monk. But it might well have been written in the local weekly paper today. To some people youth has always been "revolting"!

In 1790 William Wilberforce said, "The future is dark and unsettled," and in 1800 William Pitt said, "All around is ruin and despair"; in 1850 Wellington said, "Thank God I am spared the ruin gathering around us," and in 1880 Disraeli said, "In industry, commerce, agriculture, there is no hope." (That was when he was in Opposition.) In 1911 a gallant young soldier who had done so well in the Boer War, started a body of chaps he called The Boy Scouts, and the first time he got them together he looked at them with a smile on his face and said: "You know the times we are living in boys; well, cheer up, we'll all soon be dead!"

Pessimism is nothing new, whether about the Church or anything else. The fact is that today we know far more about what is going on, not only through the public Press, but through radio and through television. If you want to know how people behaved, go back and look through old Church records. The *News of the World* has got nothing on old Church records. But nobody saw them except the Kirk Session. And so the idea that people in the good old days were all terribly respectable and all very well-behaved and everything in the garden was lovely and people flocked to Church, simply isn't true. And so when people today say that these are terrible days we live in, it is terrible nonsense.

Not long ago I was in Rannoch and I was saying what a lovely countryside it was and how beautiful the views were and the loch was, and everything else. And then somebody said to me: "Yes, but you know, about 200 years ago up that lovely valley there about 200 McGregors were murdered by the Campbells." But nobody knew about that until about 50 years later when somebody in Edinburgh had heard it from somebody who had come down from Rannoch. But if 200 McGregors were murdered by the Campbells today we would all know by the one o'clock news. We would say: "Isn't it dreadful. Nobody ever did that when we were young." That was 200 years ago; but nobody knew. It was never broadcast, never shown on TV. And one knows today surely it is always the minority that makes the news, not the vast majority, because it *is* exceptional; and people like really exceptional things. And if you read things in the papers that seem so terrible and so awful, it's your fault and mine because that's what we want to read. We don't want to read much good news. At the same time as I received a cheque for £20,000 from The Boys' Brigade, the young boys of Scotland, gave £20,000 in a year – a tiny paragraph; when a few chaps make a fool of themselves – a whole the papers was a tiny paragraph, yet in the same paper on the front page, they had a group of revolting students! When The Boys' Brigade, the young boys of Scotland, gave £20,000 in a year, a tiny paragraph; when a few chaps make a fool of themselves a whole column. That's news, that's what people want to read; and it is our fault, yours and mine, not anybody else's; but it isn't a true picture.

All that is enough, I hope, to show what should be but isn't very obvious, that pessimism is nothing new, whether about the Church or anything else.

Each generation is faced with an equal challenge, and to some the challenge is more obvious than to others. My point is that a pessimistic Christian is a contradiction and this constant bickering against the Church should be utterly condemned, and most of all when it comes from Churchmen themselves, and there is far too much of that today.

The Church still stands as the only real challenge, to lead us on with a vision of faith, hope and love, and to bind us to Him who is the Eternal Truth, the Way and the Life.

There was a programme not so long ago on television depicting the work of the Staff College at Camberley. Towards the end of the programme the Commandant was asked what he felt were three of the best qualities that he looked for in a future leader, and he suggested the three as courage, professionalism – which includes loyalty and integrity – and compassion. No doubt he would have liked to have added a number more and I am sure in the number would have been a sense of humour, without which no one can really lead anyone. But taking these three that he chose as three of the leading qualities, I could not help considering how these would apply to the leadership that we need today.

Courage

We none of us can do without that, it is, as the late Field-Marshal Slim once put it, the greatest of all the virtues, because without it it isn't possible to practise all the others. It was the man who buried his one talent who said he did it because he was afraid. The church must never compromise because of lack of courage; it must state boldly the faith, without ever even appearing to appease passing whims or explain away the great truths or debase the moral law of God. I think it was Dean Inge who once said that those who tried to marry themselves to the present generation will find themselves widowers in the next. The Church which holds the eternal truths has no call to move with the passing whims and fashions which we call "the times", though naturally it must make itself articulate and speak in the language that can understand, without taking away the mystery, the glory of what Otto called the Numinus of the faith. Those who try too much to be "with it" today, will be "without it" tomorrow.

If, as some would have it said, the Church today is in dire straits, and even if that is true and personally I find it hard to believe, then how splendid is the challenge.

Do you remember reading of the powerful German advance after the attack of the spring of 1918 when Marshal Foch sent out that great order of the day. "My right is beaten back, my centre is weakening, the situation is excellent, I attack." And right, "We attack."

I am reminded of Warburton Lee, the first V.C. of the Second World War. Outside Narvik he reported to the Admiralty that night was coming down, a snowstorm was raging and a greatly superior enemy lay inside the Fiord. The Admiralty signalled back, "We leave the decision to you." "I attack at dawn" was his reply, and he sailed into victory and death.

"Who will go for us and whom will I send?" said the Lord.

Now is the time not to compromise but to attack.

Professionalism

Professionalism as concerned with the Church seems rather an ugly word and would seem to smack at first too much of material rather than of spiritual values; but put quite simply it can just mean knowledge of one's job, and practising that knowledge to the utmost. In other words, we must in the Church know what we believe and have a firm belief in what we are doing; and that knowledge should be put forth in a clear and concise fashion with conviction, dignity and order. Where, for example, we Ministers should be the professionals is in our specific line of vocation, and we should do and know the job to which we have been called before all else, because it is a vocation which no one else, by the very nature of our ordination, can do.

Our first – though not our only – task should be to help to make God real to men through the preaching of the Word and the ministering of the Sacraments, to feed, to comfort, to save not only the bodies, but the souls of men. In party politics, economics, and industry we Ministers are – most of us – by nature amateurs; our job is to help to make Christian politicians, economists, shop-stewards and industrialists; and too often we are tempted to tamper in matters about which we do not know enough, speaking sometimes knowing the half-truths, and not always the right half, the "hearsay" evidence, and though the voice may be the voice of the professional, the hand is the hand of the amateur.

Let me remind you of the words of my old and distinguished Professor A. E. Taylor, "Even men of high intellectual power so often make themselves merely ridiculous when they venture into fields of knowledge where they are amateurs." The Army knows of the barrack-room lawyer, the Church is beginning to hear more of the Assembly-room party politician.

Mr Harold Macmillan in his fourth volume of Memoirs says of the then Archbishop of Canterbury, "I tried to talk to him about religion . . . but he reverts all the time to politics."

Compassion

I suppose it would be true to say that among the many gifts that Christianity brought into the world not the least was the gift of compassion. The concern not just for people but for each individual person; not only do people matter, but each single person matters; each made in the image of God, however defaced that image may have become. Before we too rapidly judge or condemn, it is our duty to put ourselves into the position of others. Fr. Stanton of Holborn used to speak not with contempt but with sympathy for what he called the "undeserving poor". "God remembers that we are dust", he once said, "and you can't expect dust to be up to the mark all the time!" Here we find it emphasised so much in the difference which Christianity made. Here Christ showed us a God who really cares desperately:

> In every pang that rends the heart
> The Man of Sorrows has a part.

We find it in the parable of the sheep and the goats – "Did you really care about people in trouble?" We find it in the parable of the rich man and Lazarus. The rich man was not cruel to Lazarus, he just didn't even notice his existence, and you may remember he finished up in hell. We find it in the parable of the good Samaritan when the others just didn't notice, but he had compassion and because of that did something about it.

One is reminded of the deep concern of William Booth and how in his last speech made in 1912 – an old man now and becoming blind – he said, "When women weep as they do now I will fight; while little children go hungry as they do now, I will fight; while men go to prison, in and out, in and out, I will fight; while there yet remains one dark soul without the light of God, I will fight – I will fight to the end." And how splendidly he fought.

I suppose you could sum it all up in the Christian word for love and St. Paul's great Christian hymn of love in the Epistle to the Corin-thians.[6] It is in our compassion, in our concern for the souls and bodies of people that we will eventually surely be judged; and it is interesting to remember that what haunted William Booth most of all was the thought of children to whom the word kiss was a meaningless mystery.

These then are three of the great attributes of leadership which surely must challenge again the Church today and be in its forefront at all times — courage, professionalism — integrity — knowing the job we have each been called to do and with all our heart and strength and mind trying to do it — and compassion: "Inasmuch as you have done it unto the least of these my brethren . . .".

Our orders are clear: "It is not for you to know about dates or tmes which the Father set within His own control. But you will receive power and you will be a witness for me." For here is the message from our text:

All authority in heaven and on earth has been given to me. Go then make disciples of all nations . . . and teach them to observe all the commands I gave you. And to know that I am with you always; yes, to the end of time.

"These are the words," wrote David Livingstone at one of the most critical and frightening times of his journeys, "These are the words of a gentleman of the most sacred and strictest honour." But — and let us never forget it — these too are the words of Him who is King of Kings and Lord of Lords:

Whose praise shall never fail
Throughout eternity.

That, and not a grim pessimism, is the challenge and message to the Church in these still difficult and troublesome days — "Be not afraid, be of good cheer, I am with you always — yes, to the end of time."

[6] I Corinthians 13.

The Seven Dwarfs

Some years ago when I was thinking what I could say when asked to give another series of seven short late-night talks on television, Harry Richmond who stayed with me then, said, half jokingly and turning to the shelf in my drawing-room where ornaments of them stood, "What about the Seven Dwarfs?" The talks were to be given just after Christmas and over New Year, and I said that perhaps it wasn't a bad idea: "What about the Seven Dwarfs?" So I told the Producer, and gave him a bit of a shock when I said I was going to bring seven dwarfs with me to the studio! And there they were with me each night — the whole seven of them!

Many people have written and asked for copies of these talks which were published with an illustration of each dwarf, by kind permission of Walt Disney Productions. They quickly went out of print, and are, by special request, reprinted here.

Doc

You know what kind of chap Doc is – he always knows the answers – nothing you couldn't tell him; a real Mr Know-all.

There are a lot of people like Doc in the world, aren't there? You can't tell them anything – they know all the answers. And you and I are rather like that – at least at times! You know, when we won't listen to advice from people who are older and wiser than we are. None of us is as clever as we like to think we are at times, and we are never too old to learn. Tubby Clayton, the founder padre of Toc H, once defined an expert to me as "an ignorant man, twenty miles from home".

O there are so many things we can't understand in this world. I, for example, will never really understand the great wonder and mystery of all that Christmas means – how "He came down to earth from heaven Who is God and Lord of all". I can't understand it, but with all my heart I believe it to be true.

I believe that the good God gave us minds to use and to use them to the very limits of human thought and yet be wise enough to know when that limit is reached so that all that is left for us to do is accept and to fall down and worship.

"How could I praise if such as I could understand?"

"O the depths," said St. Paul, "of the riches both of the wisdom and knowledge of God! How unsearchable are His judgments and His ways past finding out."

So Doc teaches us that there is a limit to all our knowledge – of life and death and beyond death – and the only answer we know is the answer of faith. Or as the old hymn puts it:

I am not skilled to understand
What God hath willed, what God hath planned
I only know at His right hand
Stands one who is my Saviour

Dopey

Now here's Dopey. Doc you may remember thought he knew all the answers; but Dopey – well he hasn't a clue; he just . . . well he's just "dopey". And yet I wonder if you have noticed that he's usually the most popular of the seven dwarfs. Children like him, for example; and when it comes to likes and dislikes there's a great deal we can learn from children, isn't there? It's the childlike heart, that once we had and once we knew, that so many of us as we get older lack and secretly long for. That's one of the reasons why most people are so much nicer at Christmas time. As we remember the child in the manger, the infant of Mary, we become in the best and fullest sense of the word almost like children again, and we pull crackers and wear paper hats and join the children in their games and become more kindly and simple and trusting again – even just for a short time.

There must be some reason why children especially like Dopey, and I think that we have just seen something of that reason. For there is no pretence about him – he's just what he is – bless him – and not very much of that.

And, you know, most of us can at times be very stupid people and so in our hearts we have a secret sympathy for Dopey, and can learn a lot from him. He just doesn't pretend to be what he isn't – and when you come to think of it, there's not much harm in that. Perhaps a bit of an ass – like you and me sometimes.

But there's a comfort even in that. The blessed St. Francis you may remember called the body Brother Ass. Sometimes you and I may look and seem very stupid to the people around us – perfect asses – but then let us remember that our Blessed Lord chose an ass to carry him into the rebellious city . . . Perhaps we too, perfect asses though we may be at times, can carry Him too into rebellious places and among all sorts of people, though I hope that none of us will ever be quite such asses as to think that the cheers are for us and not for Him, whom perhaps we do not see so clearly because of the blinkers over our eyes, but whom as we try to bear other people's burdens we carry – not least at this time of year – the burden of the poor and the lonely, the cold and hungry. So as we try to bear each other's burdens we fulfil the law of Christ, and not unto us but to Him be the glory.

Happy

For the last night of the year the obvious dwarf is Happy. I don't suppose the word happy is used more often than it is at this time of the year – "A Happy Christmas", and later "A Happy New Year" have been on the lips, and will be on the lips, of more people than ever before, since . . . well since last Christmas and New Year. And it's a nice thought, isn't it, that at least for one short period of the year we should not only want other people to be happy but that we should also *say* so: and not only people we love and people we know, but all sorts of other people to whom we hardly even ever speak at other times. Just think, for example, of the number of times people will be saying "A Happy New Year" to each other – late though the night is. There's hardly a better word in all the language – except perhaps kindness and love, than the word happy. One of my best companions, before the dog I have now – my cocker spaniel Gen – was a beagle hound called "Happy" – and just for that reason.

But real happiness must always be happiness for the right things and for the right reason; happiness isn't something that comes when you look for it – it comes as the result of something. If you go out to look for happiness you will seldom find it; if you go out to seek the things that lead to happiness you will.

Have you ever thought of what the things are that really make us happy? They aren't just the things that gives us mere pleasure for the moment. They must be lasting things. And it's in that sense of the word happiness that the word "blessed" is used in the New Testament. So if you want to find out the secret of real happiness, as distinct from the mere feeling of having pleasure, you can go to what we call the Beatitudes for they begin by saying, "If you want to know who the really happy people are, well here they are." And there we find that among the really happy people of the world are those who know where to find consolation when they are sad (and perhaps even you are sad tonight amidst all your happiness because there won't be someone there tonight who was there at this time last year), and those who are gentle and kind and those who want to see right prevail, and those who show a merciful kindness to people, and try to make real peace and not just keep it at all costs, and who have the courage to stand up for what is right, and those who have no regrets and bring no unhappiness to those they love.

May we all wish each other a very happy new year in that spirit; doing the things we ought to do in the right way and for the right reasons. It won't always be easy and it won't always be painless, but it will bring us the only true happiness, and God's great gift of laughter and God's even greater gift of love of friends.

So a very Happy New Year to you and God bless you and all you love, wherever they may be.

Sleepy

Surely Sleepy is the obvious dwarf for tonight because I suppose some of you are pretty tired and were pretty late in getting to bed last night, or was it perhaps even early in the morning — in that strange way so many have starting the new year sleeping.

Have you ever stopped to think what a very large part of our lives we spend asleep — I mean really asleep in our beds, not just wandering about half-asleep. I've just worked it out that suppose I slept on an average eight hours a night, up till now I've spent nearly over twenty years asleep! Well, that makes you think, doesn't it? And I don't know how old you are but divide your age by three and you'll find how many years you have been really asleep — and that is not counting the time when you were a baby and slept most of the time — when you weren't feeding.

So, you see, sleep is a very important part of our life, isn't it? And so old Sleepy here has got something to say to us too.

Sleep is one of God's great gifts to all His creatures. Many just take it for granted; but there are some who cannot sleep well and they, if no one else, know how precious the gift is. There are some tonight who will be awake while we sleep; some there are who are working through the night. There is a rather lovely evening prayer which talks about "those who watch or work or wait this night". Don't let us forget them. But most of us will be in bed soon and, as an old professor of mine used to say, "Beds were made for sleeping not worrying." And I hope that before you go to sleep tonight you will say a little prayer – even if you haven't done so for quite a long time. It's not a bad way to begin the year – and perhaps you can keep it up all the year. Something quite simple, as you lay your head on your pillow. "Father, into Thy hands I commit my spirit" and then a word for those we love – by name. I'm sure you'll sleep better. I read the other day that during the bombing of London a woman was heard to excuse herself for having stayed quietly in bed, by saying, "Well, I reflected that God does not sleep, and there seemed to be no reason why both of us should stay awake!"

Well, I'm sure you're very tired now. Remember what the psalmist said. "God giveth His beloved sleep." Have a good sleep and God bless you and all whom you love wherever they may be.

Grumpy

Perhaps it's not a bad night to take Grumpy – just after New Year – some of you may have gone back again to work or be going back again tomorrow and you are not too pleased about it; and some of you may be reacting to the New Year cheerfulness. Of course we all get grumpy and bad-tempered at times – and none of us feel pleased about it afterwards. It's not nice being grumpy or bad-tempered at any time, is it – for whatever reason – and I'm sure most of us would like to kick ourselves for it afterwards. Mind you, there are times when we have to get cross – or pretend to be cross – and that isn't very pleasant either. And very often you can get angry with people – or pretend to be angry – just because you love them. A lot of people would have been very much happier and very much nicer people today if someone had loved them enough to have got cross with them or even punished them at times.

But once it's over we should never keep it up and nark and nag at people and forever be casting up things that should be over and done with. There is no excuse for constant bad temper and grumpiness. The Bible tells us that we should never let the sun go down upon our wrath – which means that we should "make it all up" as soon as possible. So if you have been grumpy and bad-tempered – perhaps because you were tired or someone has let you down pretty badly or you're feeling out of sorts – will you try to put it right before you go to bed – or if that's not possible, as soon as you can? You may one day leave it until it's too late. Life's too short to be grumpy or bad-tempered for long, now isn't it? There's an old song which runs something like this:

> Once when you brought me roses I scarcely
>   turned my head
> I left them where you laid them till every
>   rose was dead;
> And now I bring you roses and softly lay
>   them down
> Where you lie, quietly sleeping, in the
>   shadow of the town.

You see what I mean?

So let's try not to be grumpy or bad-tempered; and if we are don't let it last. For one thing you look, and are, so much nicer when you're smiling.

Goodnight; God bless you and all whom you love – wherever they may be.

Sneezy

Two dwarfs left . . . and here's old Sneezy. He's got a cold – has always got a cold – bless him.

And there are quite a lot of Sneezies in the world. They say, you know, that one of the the best ways of beginning a conversation with someone you don't know very well and perhaps haven't met for some time, is to say "And how is the old complaint?" – and there is nearly always a suitable answer. I once asked a man this and he thought I was talking about his wife – but usually they know you mean some illness or affliction – real or imaginary. Sometimes we can shake ourselves out of it. "I am very ill today," wrote Sir Walter Scott in his Journal, "with rheumatic headache, and a still more vile affliction which fills my head with pain, my heart with sadness and eyes with tears. I worked, therefore, all this forenoon." I love that word "therefore". But these were the days before National Health which, with all the great benefits it has brought, has also made us a nation of pill-swallowers.

And sometimes we can endure the illness with courage. When at the beginning of the last war our former Prime Minister, Lord Home, developed a very dangerous disease of the spine, he lay for two long years encased in plaster, on his back, immovable as a statue. "I never heard him once complain," said his brother Henry, "nor show any of the anger and disappointment with which most men resent such suffering. In one respect, he was pleased beyond all measure. Elizabeth, his wife, never left his side and worked for him unceasingly all through those long years – writing his letters, reading him books and papers – keeping his mind occupied and happy in his motionless body.

No wonder that whatever political party people belong to, those who know him cannot help but admire and respect him."

Well, I don't know what your complaint is. It might be very trivial, or perhaps very real; perhaps more real than others know and you're not saying very much about it. And perhaps tonight there is someone in home or hospital waiting for your prayers. You remember the old hymn:

"Comfort every sufferer watching late in pain."

And don't let us forget those wonderful and devoted nurses and doctors.

And if there are some of us tonight who feel rather sorry for ourselves, or even worried and anxious, may I leave you with the prayer that Robert Louis Stevenson wrote the night before he died – the very last thing he wrote; and perhaps it may help to carry you forward through the days and years that lie ahead:

When the day returns, O Lord, call us up with happy morning faces; and with morning hearts eager to labour; happy, if happiness be our portion, and if the day be marked for sorrow, strong to endure it.

Goodnight; God bless you all and all whom you love wherever they may be.

Bashful

I've one dwarf left and typically he's Bashful. That's the kind of fellow Bashful is; never pushing himself forward, shy, modest or perhaps with what is now called a bit of an inferiority complex.

There is, of course, a false form of bashfulness – a modest hypocrisy; you know the kind of person who, like Uriah Heep, keeps saying he's so "'umble", or the person who says he's "no use at this or not very good at that" hoping that you'll say, "Not at all, you're very good indeed." I suppose we are like that sometimes when it comes to the bit. It's called "fishing for compliments". And yet there are times when we might say oftener to people, "Well done" or "You did that jolly well" or even – and far more often than we do – "Thank you." I wish sometimes that we all did express our feelings – our nice feelings – a bit more often and a bit emphatically. It's often so simple to say; and it does sweeten life a bit and cheer people up and make life happier.

And there is a real and great form of humbleness too – the humbleness that belongs to the saints whether they have St. before their names or not, the humbleness that allows us not to think too highly of ourselves, to see our own faults and try to put them right instead of bothering so much about criticising other people's faults unless kindly, gently and courteously we try to put them right, so long as we remember that we are not too good ourselves. All the really great and good men I have been privileged to know or meet have been men of humble heart – though it perhaps hasn't always been obvious to those who only knew the "outside" of them. For real humbleness is willingness to see the best in people and so to draw the best out of them; and did not our blessed Lord "humble Himself" by becoming man "for us men and for our salvation".

Life is too short and God is too great for us to put on false airs. What are the things that really matter? Perhaps Robert Louis Stevenson got very near the mark when he said, in one of his Christmas sermons, they were "to be honest, to be kind, to earn a little and to spend a little less, to keep a few friends" – all things within the reach of the homeliest and simplest of us. And above all to have absolute trust in God and be able with Kipling to meet triumph and disaster and "treat these two impostors just the same". And so I leave you with this from the Bible, "Humble yourselves therefore under the mighty hand of God and He will exalt you in due time; casting all your care upon Him for He careth for you." And the "due time" – no one knows when:

> Suffice it if – my good and ill unreckoned,
> And both forgiven through Thy unbounding
> > grace –
> I find myself by hands familiar beckoned
> Unto my little place,
> Some humble door among Thy many mansions

And so peace at the last.

Goodnight; God bless you and all whom you love – wherever they may be.

The Seven Words

The talks on "The Seven Words from the Cross" were first broadcast by the B.B.C. on a Good Friday, with appropriate music for each Word, and later given in Glasgow Cathedral during a three-hour Service. They were first published by the B.B.C., and later in a small booklet entitled The Seven Words, *in their original form, but are slightly altered in some places here.*

The Christus Victor *by Josephina de Vasconcellos is in the Memorial Chapel in the Canongate Kirk.*

I want you to come with me and sit, as it were, around the foot of the Cross on this last hour of the three which our Lord hung there, and listen again and consider again those words spoken by Him who spoke "as no man ever spoke", the words that we now call quite simply "The Seven Last Words from the Cross"; to do, in other words, what the soldiers did who "sat down and watched Him there" — though I doubt if they heard or considered much what these words meant; and for us, just for one hour, all other things forgotten:

Father, forgive them, for they know not what they do

The place where he was crucified was, you remember, then outside the city wall; the hill may have been green but a busy road ran near for all to see, and the place seems to have been shaped like a skull. for it was called the place of the skull — Golgotha — or Latin, Calvary. It was a very mixed crowd, much larger than the crowd that at other times of the year thronged the city. And so in order that all should know just who the central figure on the three crosses was, there was a notice put up by no less a man than the local Governor of the mighty Roman Empire and written in three languages that all could read, "Jesus of Nazareth", said the notice, "King of the Jews". True, the powers-that-be tried to get the Governor to alter the notice: but he remained firm: "What I have written", he said, "I have written."

It was, as I have said, a public place; and of course it attracted the crowds.

It has never taken much to attract crowds. We read of the crowds that used to turn up at public hangings while they were still allowed in our own country; and if it were some special person the crowds of course would be all the larger and the feelings of bitter hatred and tender love all the more pronounced – the execution of Charles I in London

or Montrose in Edinburgh, for example. And so, too, great was the crowd that day outside the city wall, great in bitter hatred or curious indifference, and less great in tender pity; and being near a busy public road those who had not time to stop and stare, to gloat or weep, were able, as they passed by, to join with the others and rail at him. "You there who boasted that you could do so many impossible things, save yourself then — come down from the Cross." And there were others among the more stationary crowd whose taunting was more consistent — the priests mocking, "He saved others — but he cannot save Himself," they said. The troops of the occupying power were there on duty, and, as best they could with such a noisy rabble, keeping the peace. True to type they had had their pantomime and their bit of fun; equally true to type they showed later that gracious kindness and compassion that remains with all soldiers still.

Crucifixion was, remember, the most terrible and cruel of all punishments; its pain was ghastly. Yet look how patiently he hangs — gentle, quiet, dignified. And he "keeps on saying" something (for that is the correct translation). What is it that he says? Only one of the Gospels tells us, and, strangely almost as if it were a footnote; St. Luke tells us — and I think I know why it was St. Luke — "Father," he keeps on saying, "Father, forgive them, for they know not what they do." Forgiveness — for the unjust sentence, the cruel pain, the mocking and the jeering, the betrayal. "Was there ever," said St. Jerome, "man gentler and kinder than our Lord?" These words of comfort we can take with us now, these words of forgiveness when God knows we really do not know what we are doing; but they are words of challenge too. For there is one thing that troubles me a bit about them: suppose we DO know what we do, are doing, or perhaps propose to do. What then? Is forgiveness an easy thing, just given by simple *asking* without some effort on our part, so that we try quite honestly not to do it again? "Forgive us our sins," we pray — though perhaps not meaning it enough or often enough — or perhaps with the young St. Augustine's "but not yet": and in any case, we do not need to add "as we forgive those who sin against us". And so we come now to the Cross, praying to be forgiven and really meaning it this time.

> Wilt thou forgive that sin where I begun,
>   Which was my sin, though it were done before?
> Wilt thou forgive that sin, through which I run,
>   And do run still: though still I do deplore?
>   When thou hast done, thou hast not done,
>   For, I have more.
>
> Wilt thou forgive that sin which I have won
>   Others to sin? and, made my sin their door?

Wilt thou forgive that sin which I did shun
A year, or two: but wallowed in, a score?
When thou hast done, thou hast not done,
For, I have more.

I have a sin of fear, that when I have spun
My last thread, I shall perish on the shore;
But swear by thyself, that at my death thy son
Shall shine as he shines now, and heretofore;
And, having done that, Thou hast done,
I fear no more.[1]

Truly I say to you, today you will be with me in paradise

There were, you remember, three crosses on that first Good Friday; and the middle cross had not been meant for Him. It had been meant for the chief accomplice of the two men on either side of the central cross – a man called Barabbas. At this time of year it was the custom, it seems, for the Governor to release a prominent prisoner; and the Governor, Pontius Pilate, had decided to use his prerogative and release Jesus. For one thing, he, after a certain amount of personal investigation, had found him not guilty according to the law he administered – and Roman law was fair and just; and the last word more or less lay with the Governor. But he was an ambitious man, and it was important for his future success that he should not stir up local opinion unnecessarily; and in any case, it all seemed rather unimportant and hardly worth a brush with the local authorities and perhaps a reprimand from Rome; and so, in spite of his wife's advice and his own better judgement, he gave in. What did it matter anyway; he would soon be back in Caesarea at peace. So Jesus "suffered under Pontius Pilate", and on the centre cross, meant for Barabbas, was crucified;

[1] John Donne.

and on either side of him were two criminals, the innocent suffering with the guilty.

And the guilty joined in the jeering of the innocent. And then – was it that he heard the gracious words of forgiveness, saw the gentle dignity? "Dost thou not fear God?" he asks. "We have been justly punished but this man has done nothing wrong" – that to his friend.

And then to Jesus, "Lord, remember me when thou comest into Thy Kingdom." And our Lord's reply: "Truly I say to you, today you will be with me in paradise." There is all the difference in this world – and the next – between "This man" and "Lord remember me."

The late Canon Peter Green once pointed out that strong attraction which he, whom we now know as the penitent thief, had to Jesus on the Cross, and took as an illustration that beautiful passage in David Copperfield where, you may remember, Mr Peggotty asks Ham and Mrs Gummidge to place each night a lighted candle at the window of the upturned boat which was their home. Little Emily had run away with Steerforth and Mr Peggotty was, in love, going "through all the world" to try to find her. "Every night," he says, "as regular as the night comes, the candle must be stood in its old pane of glass, that if ever she should see it, it may seem to say 'come back, my child, come back.'" And the Cross is like that candle set by our Father's hand in the window to shine out through the darkness – "come back, my child, come back." And so we take heart and creep back trembling and, in trying to turn the key, find the door has never been bolted or barred and find what all men in their hearts seek most, forgiveness and peace. And the Cross is the "kindly light" that Cardinal Newman spoke of, to guide us home, no longer a sign of pain and sorrow but of comfort and of peace.

> And in the morn those angel faces smile,
> Which I have loved long since and lost awhile.

Paradise . . . with Him.

And if you think it is too late . . . well, it's never too late if we ask Jesus in his mercy to remember us.

> While the end is drawing near I know not mine end,
> Birth I recall not, my death I cannot foresee;
> O God, arise to defend, arise to befriend,
> O Lord all-Merciful, be merciful to me.

Mother, behold your son:
Behold your mother

As we have seen, all the people round the Cross were not hostile. Some were indifferent at first – like the soldiers; some were hostile like the chief priests; some curious like so many of any crowd are curious; but it seems that a few – and only a very few – were near and dear to him and felt as only loved ones feel for those they love; so few in fact that we know their names. "Now there stood by the Cross of Jesus His mother and His mother's sister, the wife of Cleophas and Mary Magdalane." That makes four standing near, though there were some others "standing afar off". And there was the beloved disciple John – five in all. When Jesus therefore saw his mother, and the disciple standing by whom he loved, he said to his mother, "Woman, behold your son." Then he said to the disciple, "Behold your mother."

There then is the picture – surely one of the most striking pictures in the history of the world – "The mournful mother weeping, where he lay, her dying son." His first words from the Cross remember had been for forgiveness for all because they were not really aware of what they were doing; his second to one repentant man who simply and touchingly asked to be remembered; and now to his own nearest and dearest, his mother and his best-loved friend; and by his love for St. John all human love is consecrated.

The ten other disciples had failed in the hour when they were needed most; but when the Cross was to prove victorious they all came back again and how greatly and gallantly they showed themselves to be – winning martyrs' crowns, standing before kings and governments. The Cross in its victory made cowards brave and faithless men valiant for truth – and it does so still.

I have seen it suggested that when our Lord handed the keeping of his beloved mother into the care of the beloved disciple, it was more than likely that he was also asking his mother to look after his friend. St. John was still a young man of great promise and Jesus loved him and knew the dangers that lay before him. And Jesus gave him into the hand of his mother while all the time seeming to give her into his keeping. Perhaps some of you know similar cases: "Will you look after him?" and soon you find that quite unconsciously he is looking after you. One of the very best leaders in my Boys' Club once said to me, "I don't think I've been of any use to these boys – but Oh! the good they have done me."

And often when the other disciples were busy and active, when he heard of his brother James' martyrdom, or St. Peter's imprisonment, or the journeys of St. Paul or of the erstwhile doubting Thomas going to meet a martyr's death in India, and all the rest, how he longed to be with them; but he had a charge to keep and surely he came to realise what that time of waiting and discipline and companionship of the blessed Virgin meant to him, as years after he wrote with grateful heart an old man's memories starting with what must surely be one of the greatest chapters in all history, "In the beginning was the Word . . . and the Word became flesh and dwelt among us . . . and we beheld His glory."

"Behold thy son." "Behold thy mother."

Let us again remember the precious gift of home and family life and ask ourselves whether we are helping to make it sweeter or more sour, happier or more sad. And I am sure that someone somewhere, perhaps very near, perhaps far away, on earth or in heaven, cares for you, and I wonder if you care too? Of one thing I feel sure: If more of us were to change from saying, "I couldn't care less," and were to say instead, "I must try to care more," we should find that we were better people in a better world and begin to discover what is meant by the victory of the Cross.

> Jesus, may her deep devotion
>> Stir in me the same emotion,
>> Fount of love, Redeemer kind,
> That my heart, fresh ardour gaining,
> And a purer love attaining,
>> May with Thee acceptance find.

My God, my God, why hast thou forsaken me?

It was sometime between nine and twelve in the morning when Jesus was crucified on that first Good Friday – the "third hour" they called it, the hour of the daily sacrifice of the lamb in the Temple. And then at high noon when the sun blazed at its hottest and brightest darkness came over the land and continued till three in the afternoon, the ninth hour when once again the evening sacrifice of a lamb was offered in the Temple. And today the Christian Church throughout the world still prays – "Lamb of God who takest away the sins of the world have mercy upon us, Lamb of God who takest away the sins of the world grant us Thy peace."

We have heard Jesus speak words of forgiveness for those around Him, words of comfort and reassurance to the penitent thief, and words of loving care to his blessed mother and beloved disciple. Now all was strangely dark and strangely silent. Then as darkness passes he cries out words so strange to some around him, "Eloi, Eloi, Lama sabachthani?" It was the language of his childhood uttered in his deepest agony. Some said that he must be calling for Elijah to come down and help him; the Roman soldiers may have thought that he was calling on the great Sun God Helios. But most surely knew that these were the words at the beginning of the twenty-second Psalm, "My God, my God, why hast Thou forsaken me?" And if you want to understand the full meaning of these words you should read the whole Psalm for yourself. For you will find it goes on to give almost a picture of what was actually happening at the time: "All they that see me laugh me to scorn . . . they part my garments among them, and cast lots upon my vesture"; but it ends in a great shout of triumph, "My praise shall be of Thee in the great congregation . . . for the Kingdom is the Lord's: and He is the Governor among the Nations." Well, that is one explanation – and a very possible one.

But I like to think that there is also something more and that it is not just as simple as that. This word from the Cross is surrounded with difficulty; but as Cardinal Newman once put it, "Ten thousand difficulties do not make one doubt." Jesus was perfect Man; did He not become Man for us men and for our salvation? And I like to think that there is the Man in heaven Who understands.

> In every pang that rends the heart
> The Man of Sorrow has a part.

Now there is surely no man who has not at some time in his life while retaining great faith in God – "My God, my God" – has not felt that somehow God seems to have forsaken him. "I have prayed, I have really tried, I have worked hard, I have sacrificed so much, I have . . . and yet why, my God, why?" But, as David Livingstone once put it, "A man without difficulties would be a man without a shadow." Thank God there is a Man in heaven Who understands; who can forgive out times of doubt and feelings of God-forsakenness. So this word from the Cross instead of being so mysterious is most comforting. However dark the nights of our sorrow may be – and we all have, or will yet have them, sometime – if we keep faith in God, even though for a time we feel with a feeling of desperate emptiness that he has forsaken us, the dawn will come, and with Francis Thompson we shall learn that our gloom was after all but the "shade of His hand outstretched caressingly".

> Lord should fear and anguish roll
> Darkly o'er my sinful soul,
> Thou, who once was thus bereft
> That Thine own night ne'er be left,
> Teach me by that bitter cry
> In the gloom to know Thee nigh.

I thirst

We are nearing the end of our vigil by the Cross; and perhaps because of the dark thundery skies, perhaps because the crowd had "had enough", the people around the Cross are getting fewer. His nearest and dearest would naturally stay till the end; the soldiers were on duty and could not leave. Love and duty then, as always, keep watch.

St. John, whose life from that day began anew at the foot of the Cross, alone records these words; an old man now, they must have meant much to him when first he heard them come from those pale parched lips. He had seen his Master refuse an earlier offer of a drink that would have helped to deaden the pain but yet have dimmed his clear mind. And now "I thirst" he said and straightaway one of the soldiers ran and filled a sponge full of vinegar and put it on a javelin and raised it in compassion to his lips. One of them . . . the rest said, "Let be, leave things alone; it's none of our business anyway." Oh the difference in the world between the few who run to help those in need and the others who say, "Let be."

And the soldiers' opportunity is still there today:

"Inasmuch as ye do it unto one of these the least of my brethren, ye do it unto me." He thirsts today in the lonely people, and the sad people, in the countless thousands of hungry people in now not so far distant lands, "I thirst" . . . "Inasmuch". . . . Which are you . . . the one who runs to quench the thirst or the one who says, "Let be, it's no concern of mine, I don't want to get involved"?

Or think of the cruelty still in the world today which makes "Christ within us die of thirst". Cruelty to children, drunken parents, unhappy homes – if you do not believe that such things can be, ask the societies for prevention of cruelty to children and you will be horrified, I hope; or cruelty to animals – do we put kindness to animals as one of our daily Christian duties? At least we have got societies for the prevention of cruelty to animals; but does it not seem dreadful to think that such societies should be so necessary and do so much great work as they do in a civilisation that calls itself Christian? "I thirst" . . . "Inasmuch . . . ". And still some say, "Let be." There is surely nothing worse than indifference to the pain and suffering of others, except of course the inflicting of the pain and suffering. "It is almost a definition of a gentleman to say that he is one who never inflicts pain," wrote Cardinal Newman.

Truly in his members still the Lord of all Good Life still thirsts – and not only in material things, necessary and important as they are. Men, women, and children thirst for many other things. As Peter Green put it, "The lonely thirst for companionship and the shy for friendly words, and the unattractive for consideration and for love." Do you remember the lovely story of how Bishop Bienvenu gives supper to the convict? During the meal every time the Bishop calls him Monsieur the convict's face lights up; "for," says Victor Hugo, "ignominy is athirst for respect". There are some words of the good Father Stanton that come to me over and over again, "If you want to make me a good man, speak to me as if you thought I was good and you will gain me." If you want to make a man a gentleman for goodness sake treat him as a gentleman. When the Lord Jesus Christ wanted to make some poor fishermen apostles, martyrs, saints, although they were a miserable set of men – you know what they did, they all ran away then he was in trouble – they never understood him – they left him – were very backward to believe in him – he wanted to make these men apostles, martyrs, and saints, and he said to them, "Ye are the light of the world," and they became the light of the world. And so Jesus our Lord thirsts still; do we help to quench that thirst or say, "Let be, it's not my business anyway"?

Most of us have got, or think we have got, our own burdens to bear and think they are quite enough for us to carry. But the strange thing is this, that not only in helping to bear the burdens of others too do we fulfil the law of Christ but in the doing of it our own burdens become lighter – now don't they? "I thirst" . . . "Inasmuch as ye do it unto one of these the least of my brethren, ye do it unto me." Perhaps that may be the nearest that some will ever get to Jesus; and perhaps one day we shall find that it is nearer than we had ever thought.

Strict, wounded, beaten, nigh to death
I found him by the highway side;
I roused his pulse, brought back his breath,
Revived his spirit, and supplied
Wine, oil, refreshment; he was healed:
But I had myself a wound concealed;
But from that hour forgot the smart,
And peace bound up my broken heart.

It is finished

And now we come to the two last words from the Cross – the words, "It is accomplished" and 'Father, into Thy hands I commend my spirit"; the first a loud shout of triumph, the second a quiet prayer of confidence and trust. The first two Gospels tell that there was a loud cry – only St. John tells us what the cry was – in Greek "tetelestai" – "finished". He who became Man for us men and for our salvation, had finished now the work God had given him to do. "Not the death but the will of him who freely died was well pleasing in God's sight", said St. Bernard. His work was finished, his mission accomplished – and the world would never be quite the same again; man "ransomed, healed, restored, forgiven" would never be the same again.

Have you noticed that as some people grow older they realise more and more how little they have accomplished, how the harder they try the more they seem to realise how much more they should do, and can say with Cecil Rhodes, "how much to do – how little done"? . . . In a letter I cherish from Mgr Ronald Knox, telling me that he was dying, he wrote how more and more the words came to him, "Nothing in my hand I bring"; and that has been the experience of all who have tried to serve God faithfully on earth. Only one could cry "accomplished", only one Man has ever really finished the work God gave him to do. This does not mean, I hope, that we have done nothing good, that we have not tried to serve God faithfully, and tried, too, to leave the world a better and happier place than we found it. Years of service faithfully done, whether in the Church or in parliament or city council, whether at the office, the bench, or, dearest of all, the home, can bring much-deserved joy and happiness to old age; yet even as it is true that it has ever been the saints who have been most conscious that they were sinners so those who have tried to serve God and their fellow men know best the meaning of the word, "Nothing in my hand I bring, simply to Thy Cross I cling."

Think of all the needs of the world today for clubs for young people and homes for old people and food for hungry people; and then think of the vast sums that so many store away until they die; for, as I have reminded you before, there are no pockets in a shroud. There is nothing more certain than that one day our life will end and we who brought nothing in can take nothing out; but it will not be finished. Jesus alone could say of his life on earth, "It is finished – all is accomplished."

Father, into Thy hands I commit my spirit

But these were not the last words he uttered on the Cross. Quietly now he spoke, a prayer to God, "Father," he said, "Father, into Thy hands I commit my spirit." Not one of us can say, "It is finished." But all of us can pray that prayer. It is the prayer that every mother taught her child to say last thing at night in Palestine; but Jesus added the word Father – the Son now falling asleep in his father's arms with the prayer first learnt at his mother's side. "I love to think," said a good man once, "that after the toil and stress, the agony and the shame of the Cross, when at last he resigned his soul into the Father's hands, he did it with words he had used, as a tiny boy, when he fell asleep in the Virgin's arms in the humble home at Nazareth." It is a very simple prayer and it would be a lovely thing if all mothers everywhere could teach their children from tonight to say it too; for all in fact to say it even though it may be a very long time since some of you last prayed – tonight and every night as you go to sleep – and why not too before the start of each new day. "Father into Thy hands I commend my spirit." After all, we are commending the most precious thing we have, and only to him, and to no other can we commend it.

What hurts Thee most? The rods? The thorns? The nails?
The crooked wounds that jag Thy bleeding knees?
(Can ever plummet sound such mysteries?)
It is a perchance the thirst that most prevails
Against Thy stricken flesh, Thy spirit quails
Most at the gall-soaked sponge, the bitter seas
O'erflow with this? "Nay, it is none of these."
Lord, Lord, reveal it then ere mercy fails.

Is it Thy Mother's anguish? "Search thine heart,
Didst Thou not pray to taste the worst with me,
O thou of little faith." Incarnate Word,
Lord of my soul, I know, it is the part
That Judas played; this have I shared with Thee
(So many times betrayed). "Thy prayer was heard."

So Jesus died with a prayer. But it was left to an unknown Roman soldier who was present to have the last word. "There's no doubt," said the Roman soldier, "but this was the Son of God." There was nothing more he could say – and surely nothing less. But we can, for he did not know what we know – that after that Friday came Easter Day, that "the world had died in the night", and that a new creation had begun with a new heaven and a new earth; that the Cross, the "most terrible and cruel of all punishments" has become the wondrous Cross, and Him on it – once "despised and rejected of men" the young Prince of Glory, and that that Friday when darkness fell on the face of the earth and the earth trembled, is now called Good Friday and so, as Chesterton put it, "in semblance of the gardener God walked again in the garden, in the cool not of the evening but the dawn".

> And, sitting down, they watched Him there,
> The soldiers did;
> There, while they played with dice,
> He made His Sacrifice,
> And died upon the Cross to rid
> God's world of sin.
> He was a gambler too, my Christ,
> He took His life and threw
> It for a world redeemed.
> And ere His agony was done,
> Before the westering sun went down,
> Crowning that day with its crimson crown
> He knew that He had won.[2]

[2] G. A. Studdert Kennedy.

At the request of many people I have included as an Epilogue a part of my closing Address to the 1972 General Assembly of the Church of Scotland. Thanks to the typical generosity of Major David F. O. Russell who has done so much in his quiet way, following his father's footsteps, for the Church of Scotland in general, for Iona, and not least for us in the Canongate — the complete Address was printed and sent to each Minister of the Church: then, as I do again now, I added my apologies if I had not always quoted where I should have quoted, or quoted where I should perhaps first have obtained permission.

In Christ We are all One

. . . "Things are not what they used to be," said someone to Professor Gossip once: to which he replied, "I sincerely hope not."

The first telegram I got when I was nominated as Moderator-Designate came from the Roman Catholic Cathedral in Edinburgh, and from the Abbeys of Fort Augustus and Pluscarden came invitations — invitations I gladly accepted. Moreover, Cardinal Gray and other representatives of so many denominations came to the Moderator's Reception. This new relationship and friendship between the Churches is one of the bright lights of our time, and it has tremendous possibilities for good in the future. For if Christian people cannot not only live together, but *show* too they can live together, as brethren, what hope is there for the rest of the world; and what right have we to preach a world of brotherhood for mankind if we cannot live as brothers ourselves? One of the things I found that troops could never understand was why it was thought they could do everything together throughout the week but the one thing they could not do when it came to Sunday was worship the one God together; and so they split off into various denominations and for the only time of the week were segregated. And yet it is these same troops that have set an example to us all to this very day, and not least in Northern Ireland, an example that is almost unique of discipline and comradeship that has won the admiration of us all.

The Jerusalem Bible translation from St. Paul's first letter to Timothy,[1] reads "God's family – that is the Church of the living God which upholds the Truth and keeps it safe". "God's family" – that is St. Paul's definition of the Church; and though no one would be so foolish as to think that everyone in the family always thought and felt the same – it would be a very dull family if that happened – all acknowledge one Father, children of one family. "Sir," said Dr Johnson, "the life of a parson is not easy . . . I have always considered a clergyman as the father of a larger family than he is able to maintain . . . no, sir, I do not envy a clergyman's life as an easy life, nor do I envy the clergyman who makes it an easy life."

At least when we look back on the sometimes grim times and battles of long ago – and not even so long ago – when people were willing to fight and to die, be captured and tortured, for the Faith they sincerely believed in, however much we may criticise these unhappy and sometimes cruel days, one cannot say of them that they had an easy life.

"It is," wrote Lord Macaulay in his essay on Chatham, "it is the nature of parties to retain their original enmities far more firmly than their original principles." Well, I think that this at least can be said of the present age in which we live, that we are trying to forget our ancient enmities while trying also to keep our principles, provided they do not become or remain our prejudices. As Arthur Stanton once put it, "So many waves, one ocean, so many stars, one radiant heaven. Many flocks, one shepherd . . . three persons, one God. That they may be one as we are one."

The days of re-union may still be distant but at least it means that we are a Church that is looking ahead, moving forward, *reformata sed reformanda*, moving not with the times, *if* by "the times" we mean trying to please every passing whim and fancy – there are some things

[1] Timothy 3: 15.

that cannot be moved for the Church is the guardian of truths that are eternal – "Remember that Truth does not depend on our approval or disapproval. We are at stake; not the Truth. The compass is not less true when some sailor does not trust to it" as Dr Charteris once said – but moving none-the-less in a language that man can understand so that eternal truths remain. It means not looking backwards to old feuds and battles long ago, but forwards to new horizons; it means "attempting new heights, and bringing even dreams to birth". Of this I feel sure – and there are not many things about which I can feel sure – that there are no Roman Catholics in Heaven and no Episcopalians, no Baptists, Methodists, and no Presbyterians; there are only the children of the one Father in Heaven. We pray that God's Will may "be done on earth as it is in Heaven"; who then can say unity doesn't matter if we mean what we say in our prayers? . . .

It is well to remember that the Scottish Divines had never lost the vision of a single and universal Church upon earth. You will find it in Knox: "As we believe in one God, Father, Son and Holy Ghost, so do we most constantly believe that from the beginning there hath been, now is, and to the end of the world shall be, one Kirk . . . which Kirk is Catholic, that is, universal." You will find it in Melville, in Samuel Rutherford, in Archbishop Leighton. For though they never excluded their own enemy Rome and acknowledged their baptism as valid, they longed for re-union – albeit on their own terms.

Samuel Rutherford, as John Buchan has reminded us, who was commonly known as an "affectionate" preacher, taught "the loveliness of Christ, for thirty years, without ever perceiving the unloveliness of intolerance". Compare that with the statesmanship and charity of the great Thomas Chalmers: "Who cares about the Free Church," he said, "compared with the Christian good of the people of Scotland . . . be assured that the moral and religious well-being of the population is of infinitely higher importance than the advancement of any sect. . . ."

From our student days some of us owe so much to two great Churchmen, men in some ways so different, each with so much to give; Dr Charles Warr, now in the Church Triumphant, and Lord MacLeod, still in the Church Militant – and sometimes very militant! . . . We Edinburgh students of our generation look back to these early days of Toc H in Edinburgh, as Dr Roy Sanderson too can tell you, where we used to meet each week to "recharge our batteries", and go out again, keeping before us what were known as the four points of the compass, four points I have ever tried to keep before me, however inadequately. And the first of these points of the compass are the words "to love widely", the second, "to think fairly", the third, "to witness humbly", and the fourth, "to build bravely".

First – to love widely. There are few more beautiful pictures in the story of the early Church than that of the beloved Apostle St. John, an old man now, borne through the streets of Ephesus, saying to all as he passed, "little children, love one another". (For "Love is the abridgement of all theology" as St. Francis de Sales once said.) Among the many apostles of love since then, may I mention two whose centenaries we remember especially this year[2] – one who like those who bore his name before him and have borne it since, and who was never afraid to speak the truth as he saw it, but always spoke the truth in love – the great Norman McLeod. . . . "Love is the only way along which the whole world may reach greatness." . . . The other – so shamefully treated by the General Assembly of his day – John McLeod Campbell, who, as we all know, was deposed as a heretic by the General Assembly because he taught that God loved all his children and not just a chosen few. . . .

It is that constant lack of Christian love which may suffer long but is always kind, that one so often looks for in vain in the story of our Church as contained in the records of its history. Not that that love has not often been there, but it has so often been unrecorded. The greatest names in our Church's history are in many cases those who have no memorial except the love of their people; whose voices have seldom been heard in the Courts of the Church, and whose deeds have seldom been recorded except in the hearts of simple folk: though these more than any other is the Church "all glorious within"; "merciful men whose righteousness hath not been forgotten". . . .

In that book about E. W. Tennant,[3] who was killed, like so many others, so young, in the First World War, and like so many others who, had they lived, would have helped to make this country great ("Bimbo" Tennant, of whom a private soldier was to write to his father, a former Lord High Commissioner, "when danger was greatest his smile was loveliest") – he tells of an old priest whose hat was worn and old "from being so constantly taken off to a great many inconspicuous people". . . .

[2] 1972.   [3] Edward Wyndham Tennant: A Memoir.

To those who know a little of Christian (as distinct from merely Church) history, probably the most moving of all the reflections it brings is not the thought of the great events and the well-remembered saints, of those innumerable millions of entirely obscure faithful men and women, every one with his or her own individual hopes and fears and joys and sorrows and loves – the sins and temptations and prayers – ones every whit as vivid and alive as mine are now. "For they left not the slightest trace in this world, not even a name, but have passed to God utterly forgotten by men. Yet each of them once believed and prayed, as I believe and pray, and found it hard and grew slack and sinned and repented and fell again. Each of them worshipped at the Eucharist and found their thoughts wandering and tried again, and felt heavy and unresponsive and yet knew – just as real and pathetically as I do – these things," as Gregory Dix has written.[4]

Love doesn't always mean agreeing with, but it does mean always understanding:

> There's a wideness in God's mercy
> Like the wideness of the sea
> There's a *kindness* in His Justice
> Which is more than liberty.

The new "Jesus movements", the new Festivals of Light with their emphasis on love help to illustrate the words of St. John of the Cross: "Where there is no love put love in and you will draw love out." But to love our Lord surely means also to obey Him, to recognise His Divinity as well as His Humanity, and to serve His Church from within it and not just from outside.

Many may become, sometimes quite understandably, impatient with the Church as organised and may feel somehow it has lost its sense of proportion: Remember G. K. Chesterton:

> The Christian Social Union was very much annoyed
> It seems we have a duty which we never should avoid
> And so we sang a lot of hymns to help the unemployed.

But let us remember that it is only through the Church that the Gospel has ever reached us and only through the Church can it reach the ages far ahead. As William Temple once said, "You will do more service to the cause of Christ by bringing in what reality you can into its life than you can ever render by staying outside and doing what seems possible to you, or you and your friends, in isolation."

[4] From *The Shape of the Liturgy*, by Dom Gregory Dix.

And it is He who has commanded us to "do this" in remembrance of Him. Dom Gregory Dix when commenting on the command "to do this" added, "Was ever command so obeyed?" . . . "Let us love one another," wrote St. John;[5] but added, "and love means following the commands of God".

And the second point of the compass was to think fairly.

We must learn to see the other person's point of view without necessarily agreeing with it; and recognise that sincerity and conviction are not restricted only to ourselves. "Go through life," said Sir James Barrie to the students of St. Andrews, "without ever ascribing to your opponents motives meaner than your own. Nothing so lowers the moral currency; give it up and be great."[6]

How can we be expected to think fairly unless we at least *attempt* to know all the facts?[7] This is, I venture to suggest, where some of us who are Ministers can sometimes make such fools of ourselves when we sometimes try to become party politicians and become merely puppet politicians; and neglect too often, as a consequence, the vocation to which we were called, and for which we were ordained; because it is a vocation which no one else, by the very nature of our ordination, can do. "It is the duty of the clergy," said W. R. Maltby once, "to feed the sheep and not to amuse the goats"; as a leading Churchman[8] once reminded us, "parsons are not ordained to teach adolescents how to play table-tennis . . . and there is no Catholic way to play billiards". I am not saying that we should not at times do these things; but our first task surely should be to make God real to men through the preaching of the Word, and not just by words, the ministering of the Sacraments which we alone can do, and the otherwise often neglected care of the sick, the lonely, the aged and the children. In politics, economics and industry we may too have our parts to play – no one could deny that – but there we are by nature amateurs; our main vocation is to make *Christian* politicians, economists, shop stewards, and industrialists. . . . "I am more and more of a mind," wrote Robert Baillie, "that Churchmen, be they never so abill, are unhappie statesmen."

We too often confuse prejudices and principles and criticise, per-

[5] 2 John, v. 6.   [6] *Courage*
[7] "I believe that no man has a right to criticise who has not first learned the ability to admire" – Anthony Chenevix-Trench, Headmaster Bradfield, Eton and Fettes.   [8] The Late Cardinal Heenan.

haps quite rightly, what some country does, yet fail to criticise what other countries even within our own Commonwealth are doing in a similar or even worse way.

And so in our relations too between other Churches. In beginning to know each other better we are beginning to think more fairly as we are beginning to love more widely. As Barclay Baron once put it, "to conquer hate would be to end the strife of all ages; but for men to get to know one another is not difficult and that is half the battle".

The third point of the compass was to witness humbly.

Satan, says the legend, was cast out of Heaven not because he was promiscuous (though for all I know he may have been) but because he was proud. We are surely right to not in any way condone promiscuity, but sometimes we forget that there can be even worse sins than the sins of the promiscuous society, and there are the sins of the spirit — sins of jealousy, of envy, of covetousness, of cruelty, and of pride.

Surely St. Augustine was right! "No one is known to another so intimately as he is known to himself, and yet no one is so well known to himself that he can be sure as to his own conduct on the morrow." That in itself should give us sufficient cause to each day witness humbly. In the well-known words of Oliver Cromwell in the letter to the General Assembly of the Church of Scotland, in 1650: "I beseech you, in the bowels of Christ, think it possible you may be mistaken."

And, finally, to build bravely.

We can look back at the history of our Church in anger, in affection, in sadness, and in rejoicing, with pride and with humility; and we have reasons for all these moods. We can learn from the past the mistakes of the past, the cruelty of the past, the courage of the past, the charity of the past. We can look back and learn, but we must not live in the past but in the present as we look to the future. We can see great men who in days gone by have with great courage led us on and pray God still lead us on in the Church militant — some of our own branch, others in other branches of that one Holy Catholic Church to which we all belong. As John Buchan once put it,[9] "Slowly, painfully, the Church rid itself of certain sinister heritages; it shed the mediaevalism which made it a rival of the State; it abandoned its narrow Scriptural literalism; it learned that toleration was not a pagan voice but a Christian virtue, and that the path of unity didn't lie

[9] From *The Kirk in Scotland*.

through a bleak uniformity." But all these lessons would have been in vain had not a vision of the peace and felicity of a united Jerusalem survived among good men in each generation, even when their conscience demanded a further disruption. These men, moving down through the ages are many of them great figures, attaining often to heroic stature, men who had the making of their country in their hands; for the history of Scotland is largely the history of her Church . . . men like the great John McLeod of Govan – "who being dead yet speaketh" – men like Chalmers, whom John Buchan once described as "the greatest constructive mind that the Scottish Church has produced, and one of the noblest figures in any Church" – and few would deny that description – back to the days of the Moderates and the Evangelicals, to the hillside preachers and the fireside prayers, back to the early Reformers, with a passion not, as they claimed, to create a new Kirk, but to reform the old. For the old came not only from Iona where St. Columba was "both Prince and Priest" and who, on another Isle, like John on Patmos, had visions of peace among men, not only from St. Ninian, not only from St. Martin, but back to that first upper room in Jerusalem where on that first day of Pentecost it all began; the brave small band that went out "conquering and to conquer", and yet to be more than conquerors, for with them they carried the message not of bitterness or hatred but of love; not of tears and sorrow, but of a "peace that passes understanding".

And we, "compassed about with so great a cloud of witnesses", are all a part of that procession.

INDEX